DAVID R. MAINS

NEVER TOO LATE TO

DREAM

Mainstay Church Resources

ver Too Late to Dream

Vision of Mainstay: In this sight and sound culture, our holy task is to
help pastors help people grow on Sundays and beyond. To support this
vision, Mainstay provides practical tools and resources, including the
annual 50-Day Spiritual Adventure, the Seasonal Advent Celebration, and
our website: www.teamsundays.org.

Printed in the United States of America
ISBN 1-57849-290-4

03 04 05 06 07 08 09   10 9 8 7 6 5 4 3 2

MAINSTAY
*Leading the Team for
Life-Changing Sundays*

Visit our website: **www.teamsundays.org/adventure**

CONTENTS

I want to express my appreciation to Cathy Davis and to Chariot Family Publishing (now Chariot Victor Publishing) for allowing me to quote extensively from Tales of the Resistance.

In the chapters that follow, you will get acquainted with some of the characters in the Tales. *They will whet your appetite to meet others who appear in the* Tales of the Kingdom, Tales of the Resistance, *and* Tales of the Restoration, such as these:

The Carnival Daughter
The Sewer Rat and the Boiler Brat
The Girl Named "Dirty"
The Baker Who Loved Bread
The Two Noisy Knights
The Apprentice Juggler
The Faithless Ranger
and many more

These tales were written for children of all ages. Like all good stories, they teach lessons of great value. If you would like to get to know these other characters or read more of the Kingdom Tales trilogy, see pages 191 and 192 at the end of this book.

INTRODUCTION

How did I get myself into this? I mused as I got dressed that Monday morning several years back. *My schedule for this week is already too full. Why did I agree to take an entire day to talk with an industrial psychologist?*

Then I remembered. A board member had suggested this meeting. That's what it was. He knew a professional who had offered his services free of charge to several executives of Christian ministries. This psychologist had said he would be glad to give a day of his time to talk with those leaders about their dreams. Possibly he could be of help in seeing their visions find fulfillment. For him, that would be a way to use his gifts in the Lord's work. But no one took him up on his offer. "Would you be interested?" my board member wanted to know. He could arrange a meeting.

What was I to say? At the time, our ministry was struggling. The board wasn't confident we would make it. The reasons are too complex to go into. But our staff had cut back our already thin work force. Now all of us had more to do than we could handle. Looking back on that time, I recall it was like trying to outrun a bullet. Could we race fast enough. . . and for long enough? We might make it. Might! . . . But the odds weren't good.

This is ridiculous, I thought as I drove to where we would be meeting. *I don't have time for dreams anymore. My present ministry has gone about as far as it's ever going to go. My visions seem to have come to an abrupt halt. End of the line, buddy! Face it, David, you don't have the luxury of dreaming.*

Our meeting was at a private Chicago club. I wasn't paying—the psychologist I hadn't yet met was. The conference room was large and luxurious, quite a contrast to the setting of the staff get-together I had held the Friday before. Around the table in our small lunchroom, I had outlined to my key workers our financial status. We had coffee, but not served from a silver pot. Now, in this new setting, four of us sat around a gorgeous table that could comfortably accommodate a dozen. A tray of sweets came with the coffee service. Then the gentleman who had invited us took over and explained the agenda to me, to my board member, and to one of my top executives.

"It's my privilege to have you as guests. I want very much to use my gifts for the Lord. But sometimes at church it seems my only choices are ushering, teaching a junior high class, or singing in the choir. My best skills relate to working with executives. So, again, thank you for allowing me to see if I can be of help."

I warmed to his approach and soon felt at ease. Then, as he continued, I heard an expression I didn't understand. "Hopefully," he said, "we'll break glass before long. That's one of my desires."

"Break glass," I stopped him. "I don't know what that means."

"Most people don't see their dreams fulfilled—their

visions become reality—because their thinking has become restricted," he explained. "It's like being in a great room such as this one, only with a glass ceiling overhead. You can see above you, but you can't get into that new horizon unless you break the glass ceiling and open up for yourself that greater world."

"Will I know when that happens?" I questioned.

"You'll know when we get to such a place," he responded. "Then you'll have to decide what to do. Hopefully we can break glass a couple of times today. That's one of the gifts I can give you. But first, tell me what the Lord has called you to do, David. What's he laid on your heart? What are his dreams for you?"

Now it was my turn to talk. But it wasn't as easy as I had thought. Again, I wasn't in a dreaming mood. We were operating with a "survive another week" mindset. My world was shutting down, not expanding. Still, I tried to put the immediate aside and talk about what the Lord had laid on my heart in the earlier days of my ministry. Mostly, that related to seeing the church come alive.

Words came out about our being an organization that was a servant to the church, that encouraged pastors, that helped laypeople discover and use their gifts even as this man wanted to do. As a ministry, we dared to believe that Christians cared deeply about seeing another great spiritual awakening—a revival of faith that would begin in individual lives and then affect marriages, enhance family relationships, touch the workplace, build up our churches, beautify our cities, and make our nation strong in every way.

9

As time passed, I told my host about our annual 50-Day Spiritual Adventures, how they were tools for accelerated spiritual growth, that those who participated could measure their progress, and how the number of individuals and churches involved had grown year by year.

"Are your Adventure materials offered overseas?" he asked.

"To a limited degree," I replied. "We've done extensive experiments in India with over a hundred thousand participants. The materials have been translated into Spanish and also tested in . . ."

"I would think they could be even more effective overseas than they are here," he suggested. "From my observations, missions organizations are better at evangelism than they are at discipleship. Your Adventure journals would be perfect in places like Nigeria, the Philippines, Honduras..."

"But you don't understand," I interrupted. "We're scrambling just to make it in North America. We struggle to meet budget. I don't have the luxury of talking about overseas projects. It's hard enough. . . ."

"Hold on," the psychologist said loudly. "I believe we have just come to a glass-breaking time. You agree there's a great need for materials like these overseas, but your mind is conditioned to go only so far. Then it bumps into a ceiling of your own making. You're not dreaming new possibilities because you're accustomed to a ceiling where it is now. The question is whether you're willing to break glass so we can at least explore various options and their ramifications."

It's amazing that even now as I write, I can still feel the tension of that moment. *Why take time to explore what isn't reality?* I wondered. *This new territory is out of bounds for me.*

My host didn't give up. He reasoned, "Maybe the overseas market is the key to future growth for you."

I didn't want to hear that.

"Maybe overseas expansion could resolve your money problems," he continued.

I knew it wouldn't. Missions projects only added to the expense column.

"Can we at least talk about it?" he wondered.

Silence.

"Well now, are we going to break glass, or aren't we?"

"OK," I finally acquiesced. "Let's go for it."

An hour and a half later, we were at another "glass-breaking" juncture, another ceiling to be shattered, and another jumbling up of all my familiar thought patterns.

Finally it was lunchtime. Thank the Lord! I'd try to get my head reoriented and think through the ramifications of what was being discussed.

Half an hour after lunch we came to another glass ceiling that needed to be shattered. *So, why not*, I thought, *let's bust it out!*

But fifteen minutes later I had a headache built for a rhinoceros!

"I need to stop," I confessed. "My normal thinking circuits are so hopelessly rewired, I can't function without great strain."

"Then I suggest we quit," the psychologist said. "This has been a good day. I believe I've given you a great gift. It happened faster than I thought it would. So I'm pleased. Again, thank you for letting me exercise my gift."

I'm glad I've made him so happy, I thought, recognizing the irony in the situation.

But looking back on that meeting, I realize it was one of the best things that ever happened to me. I've been involved in a lot of brainstorming sessions, but this one literally changed my life.

In the ensuing months and years, our ministry went through an amazing turnaround. And best of all, now I'm dreaming again. Not my dreams—I believe they're the Lord's dreams for me.

Taking a cue from my own experience, I think a large percentage of Christians have glass ceilings that need to be shattered. I suspect this is so because their faith appears to be suffocated. They function with less spiritual breathing room than they used to. At one time, they had dreams of what their lives could mean for God, but somewhere along the line those dreams died. How sad. Maybe you can identify with believers like that.

The problem is not something new to this generation. For example, Scripture tells us Gideon had a similar experience. When the angel of the Lord first appeared, he greeted Gideon with these positive words, "The Lord is with you, mighty warrior" (Judges 6:12).

According to Judges 6:13, Gideon replied, "But sir . . . if the Lord is with us, why has all this happened to us?"

Gideon was referring to the oppression of the Jews by the Midianites. He wasn't exactly in a dreaming mood either. But in the encounter that followed, some glass ceilings were broken right there near the winepress where he had been threshing wheat. And when Gideon said, in essence, "God, I want your dreams for me to be my dreams as well," it was a new and wonderful day for Israel.

That's what I want for myself and for you: that we dare to dream again. It's never too late to dream God's dreams for us. We can break through the barriers that hold us back and become—in this opportune time when God pours out his Spirit—those sons and daughters who prophesy, those older folks who dream dreams, and that younger generation which can still embrace visions (Joel 2:28).

CHAPTER ONE
LET GOD HEAL
YOUR PAINFUL PAST

H ero was afraid.

He watched the Ranger hold a burning torch to the ring of stones that circled the place of the Great Celebration. The Sacred Flames ignited with a w-o-o-O-O-O-SH, lifting the hems of the blue robes of the protectors of Great Park, who stood as sentries around Inmost Circle. The silver insignia of the Rangers caught the light and flashed in the outer circle around the rim of fire.

Tonight he would leave these friends, leave Mercie and Caretaker, leave these woods, these dear fields, leave everything, in the world he had come to love. *Well, almost everything,* he reminded himself: What he loved most in the world was the King and to be a King's man and to do the King's work.

And the voice of that King, the most beautiful of men, had spoken inwardly only this morning: *It is time. It is time to begin the restoration of the Kingdom. I need a King's man with a hero's heart. Will you come?*

This is how my wife, Karen, and I begin our book *Tales of the Resistance.* It's written for children of all ages to enjoy. I'll use sections from these tales to develop the themes of the chapters that follow in this book.

Far off, Ranger horns sounded from the watchtowers that guarded Deepest Forest. *Croi-croi!* Come-come! *Croi-croi!* Come to Inmost Circle! Come to the solemn assembly!

Hero watched as the people he loved made entrance, passed through the Sacred Flames and became real. He watched Amanda step into the fire a ragtag tomboy and step out a beautiful, graceful princess. He watched the unhappy woman who had been the orphan keeper's assistant become someone with a mother's smile for all the children, who ran to hug her. He saw Caretaker become Ranger Commander.

How can I ever go? thought Hero. *How can I leave all this?* But he had heard the voice of his King: *Come, Hero. It is time.* And he knew he must go.

A DREAM IN YOUR HEART

Like young Hero in this tale, I assume you know a little of what it's like to have the King place a dream in your heart. And not just any dream—His dream. Being able to dream God's dreams for us is a marvelous privilege.

This is not the same as personal dreams for a bigger house . . . a better job . . . more acclaim. God's dreams for us involve service—valorous service on behalf of His Majesty.

What dreams has God placed in your heart?

• Maybe you were first in your family to meet the

King, and you dreamed of sharing this experience with all those you loved. Or . . .

- You dreamed of studying the Bible and someday being able to share its marvelous truths with people in need. You could picture yourself giving of your faith and delighting the Lord with your love for Him. Or . . .

- You dreamed of starting a youth group where "King's love" could be experienced by guys and girls who were looking for it in all the wrong places. Or . . .

- You dreamed about helping plant a church in a growing subdivision where you purchased a new house. Or . . .

- You wanted to establish a new congregation in the inner city. I dreamed that dream once. In my mind I could see a church of whites and blacks, Hispanics and Asian Americans, all worshiping together, modeling the oneness in the body that Christ prayed for.

- Maybe your dreams concerned another country. Your aspirations might have been so expansive that they required others to work alongside you.

17

How have you responded to the dreams God has given you? Perhaps you've felt the way Hero did as he anticipated going forth to serve the King.

   . . . This solemn assembly had been hurriedly gathered for the Rite of Adoption, for no lad could go back into the Enchanted City an orphan. Orphans belonged to the evil Enchanter. Hero must be someone's son; he must have proof of parentage to protect him.

   Dread filled his soul. He thought of the darkness of Enchanted City, where the citizens worked by night and slept by day. He remembered Burning Place where the dead were burned: all who had died of weariness, of hunger, of heartsickness.

   In his memory, he saw fire burning the pyre that held his mother's body. (She had always said, "There is a King. A real King!") Death drums began to beat in his mind: *oo-mb-pha . . . oo-mb-pha . . . oo-mb-pha-din*. Visions of Burners with hot brands and smoldering pokers flashed. He heard the blows of the Breakers. The song of the Naysayers, *nay-nay-nay, nay-nay-nay, nay-nay-nay*, clutched his heart with icy fingers.

   He remembered Branding—himself a screaming five-year-old—and how the hot iron had seared his cheek. For the first time in many months, Hero touched the scar. Here, in this place among these people, he was Hero, loved by many. In that terrible place, he was nothing but scum. The people of Enchanted City would point and jeer in the old way—Scarboy! Scarboy!

   S-C-A-R-B-0-Y!!

   Suddenly, Hero heard a scream rise out of

Enchanted City and fall with a paralyzing moan in his own soul. He raised up his head, startled. It was more than memory. Hero knew it was the voice of the evil Enchanter from the dark midst of the Dagoda, with his fiery head thrown back, with fire priests dancing and their ceremonial bells *jangling: jchang-jchang-jchang.*

S-C-A-R-B-O-Y!!

Hero cowered, standing outside the Circle of Flames. His heart felt like stone. The hot eye of the Enchanter had found him, here in his fear. How could he follow the King if he kept hearing this loud and terrible cry? He would be vulnerable, alone.

"Oh, Mercie," the lad whispered to the old, old woman beside him. "I'm afraid. How will I ever find the King? You know I'm not good at recognizing disguises. I can *feel* the Enchanter's hot eye, and hear the *nay-din-nay-din* of Enchanted City, and remember the brands and the blows and the stink of Burning Place."

The old woman took his hand, and Hero felt the strength of her grasp. Mercie smiled. "Hero, fear is ever the Enchanter's ally. Have you forgotten your own powerful weapons?"

A painful past can often inhibit our dreams. Perhaps you've experienced pain such as . . .

- A split of close friends within a church

- The failure of a spiritual leader you trusted

- Betrayal by a Christian friend you went to for

19

help, who told others about your problem

- An experience where you tried your best to serve the Lord, but you failed

- Embarrassment by a harsh authority figure

- Criticism from class members you were teaching

- Having your best efforts sabotaged by a ruling board

- Being left for another by your mate

- Horrible memories of childhood abuse just now starting to surface

For me, after feeling I had failed in my inner city efforts, I was afraid to open myself to dreaming again for well over a decade. I ministered assuming something bad would happen that would undermine whatever I tried to do. My leadership style was careful and guarded. But I found in time that it wasn't nearly as much fun serving the Lord like that. I still wanted to believe he had a dream for me that fit perfectly into what he was doing in his world.

Maybe that's how you feel. A cacophony of voices from your past screams in your mind, "Your real name is Scarboy . . . or Scargirl. You'll never make it when it

20

comes to serving this King of yours!"

If we're not careful, we adopt the names others give us and forget that God calls us to be heroes, that in his eyes we are not destined to be frightened but instead are meant to be men and women of valor.

"Come on, David," you say. "It's a tale for children you're referring to, remember? This is the real world, not Great Park and Enchanted City."

BORN TO BE A HERO

Then let me briefly review a tale you know about another young man born to be a hero. When we first meet him, he's covertly threshing grain at the bottom of a winepress. He's there because he's hiding from Midianite invaders who annually come in great numbers to strip the land bare.

Near this unlikely place to look for a fearless warrior, an angel appears to Gideon and says, "Mighty hero, the Lord is with you!" Our candidate for fame must have first thought the words were spoken in sarcasm, because he responds somewhat snidely, "If the Lord is with us, why has all this happened to us?" (Judges 6:13 NLT). *We're an impoverished people barely scraping together a living. Look at us: we're a pitiful lot. And what's happened to all the great miracle help from God our ancestors all talked about? Let's face it. We've been divinely abandoned!*

Talk about a painful personal past! Israel's glorious history only served to make the nation's current calamities all the more intolerable.

21

Verses 14 and 15 say, "The Lord turned to him and said, 'Go in the strength you have and save Israel out of Midian's hand. Am I not sending you?'

"'But Lord,' Gideon asked [realizing now that his visitor was someone truly special], 'how can I save Israel? My clan is the weakest in Manasseh, and I am the least in my family.'" *We can't lick anybody. Maybe you didn't notice, but we're hiders, not fighters. Everything about my past prompts me to laughingly reply, "No can do!"*

Listen, Gideon, dreaming God's dreams for us often requires letting go of painful past experiences.

I've had to say those words more than once to myself: *Listen, David Mains, dreaming God's dreams for us often requires letting go of painful past experiences.*

And I repeat the words for you, whatever your name is. Dreaming God's dreams for us often requires letting go of painful past experiences.

At first it appeared that Gideon had no intention of coming out of hiding—to say nothing of daring to dream again. That, of course, left a major question to be discussed. How then would the people of God be delivered from Midian?

The answer is that Gideon needed to be healed of his painful memories in order to do his divinely assigned job. He would have to learn to break through this barrier that held him back. The Lord needed to help his servant let go of a negative past identity, so he could assume a positive new one. Fortunately, God is exceptionally good at this. It's one of his specialties, isn't it—healing broken people of one kind or another?

Notice how the Lord gently and incrementally led Gideon along. "I will be with you," he promised, "and you will strike down all the Midianites together" (verse 16).

The prophecy seemed preposterous, but it did actually happen:

> Gideon replied, "If now I have found favor in your eyes, give me a sign that it is really you talking to me. Please do not go away until I come back and bring my offering and set it before you."
>
> And the Lord said, "I will wait until you return."
>
> Gideon went in, prepared a young goat, and from an ephah of flour he made bread without yeast. Putting the meat in a basket and its broth in a pot, he brought them out and offered them to him under the oak.
>
> The angel of God said to him, "Take the meat and the unleavened bread, place them on this rock, and pour out the broth." And Gideon did so. With the tip of the staff that was in his hand, the angel of the Lord touched the meat and the unleavened bread. Fire flared from the rock, consuming the meat and the bread. And the angel of the Lord disappeared. When Gideon realized that it was the angel of the Lord, he exclaimed, "Ah, Sovereign Lord! I have seen the angel of the Lord face to face!"
>
> But the Lord said to him, "Peace! Do not be afraid. You are not going to die."

Read the rest of chapter 6 and chapter 7 of Judges on

your own and see how the Lord carefully affirmed Gideon one step at a time until, before you know it, the giant task was completed and young Gideon truly had become a hero to his people.

Sooner or later the "spiritual hero" side of all of us should also begin to emerge. This can happen when a church, which needs to be more than a ward for the walking wounded, points the way to healing and helps us move forward. If that doesn't occur, we are a sad bunch indeed. We really can't be part of the Lord's magnificent dream for this world if we are all held back by painful memories.

Let's return to our young fictional Hero. He has heard the voice of his King speak in his heart that it is time to return to Enchanted City to begin the restoration of the kingdom. Painful memories from childhood, including the fact that he was called Scarboy, make this a hard assignment for him to accept—just like Gideon.

> "Ranger initiate!" called out Commander. "Stand forth for Revealing!"
>
> With a pounding heart, Hero obeyed. He had always longed to be a Ranger, a protector of Great Park, but never, never had he felt so unworthy as at this moment.
>
> Kneeling and bowing, Hero felt Ranger Commander's hand placed firmly on his head. The voice which always filled him with awe spoke above him.
>
> "Tonight we are gathered to induct the lad Hero into the corps of Rangers, protectors and watch-

keepers for the King. What is your pleasure?"

The blue-cloaked men and women spoke as one: "Let the ceremony begin!"

The awful first question was asked: "Does anyone know just cause why this one, Hero, should not be invested with the office of Ranger?"

Each Ranger in the circle answered in turn.

"I do not," said the first.

"Nor do I," called out the next.

The lad kneeled in an agony of suspense. He longed with all his being for this office, but he wished someone would speak to his unworthiness before he shamed them all by being a faithless Ranger.

"Nor I—nor I." And so, round the circle came the pledges of faith. Hero could hardly believe that not one Ranger would show just cause that he was unworthy.

Then the second awful question: "Do you, initiate, hold just cause against yourself?"

Hero sighed deeply. Revealing demanded honesty. Lifting his head, he looked into Commander's eyes, "Sire, I—I am afraid. I am afraid of the task at hand."

A murmur went up from the blue-cloaked circle. A voice cried, "No just cause! Even the most courageous fear the unknown task!"

Hero gulped. "But Sire, I—I doubt. The mettle of the powers is unknown to me. I fear its weakness against the force of Enchanted City."

Another voice cried, "Power is always untested until it has been tried. No just cause!"

Hero spoke one last time. "Sire, my seeing is dim, and the voice of the Enchanter is near."

25

Ranger Commander answered, "Dim sight is cured by choosing to see. We hear the voice of whomever we allow near. No just cause. Stand forth."

Hero rose from his knees. Ranger Commander called above his head, "What is the pleasure of this company? Shall we induct this Hero, once of Enchanted City, now of Great Park, for the task at hand?"

A hurrah went up from the circle of Rangers, followed by another larger shout from the crowd standing beyond. "To vows! To vows!"

Hero's heart swelled with this honor. He would be a Ranger. He would fight for the King. He would give his forever pledge to protect the Kingdom, to be faithful. "To the King!" he shouted.

"To the King!" all shouted back.

"To the Restoration!"

The kingdom—that's the big picture too many in the church have lost sight of today. It was Christ's key message. He talked about the kingdom again and again, his present and future kingdom.

Christ's kingdom, or kingship, is wherever he is recognized as King. His will is obeyed, and subjects reap the benefit of his rule.

Heaven is that way. All subjects there bow before Christ as King. In heaven all are obedient to his will and reap great benefits. So heaven is the kingdom, or kingship, of Christ.

But the kingdom is here as well. When we bow to Christ as Lord and obey his will, we are the ones who benefit as we live under his gracious kingship. In fact, Christ taught us to pray, "Your kingdom come, Your will be done on earth as it is in heaven" (Matt. 6:10).

Kingdom people believe in restoration—in release from oppression for the people of God. It is the King's ultimate dream for the world that we cherish.

Now is the time to dream great dreams again for our Lord. His return may be soon. Can we be King's men and King's women in this day? Can we put the pain of our past experiences aside? It is important to recognize that:

- The person who hurt you may never ask forgiveness.

- The marvelous ministry job you did may never be recognized.

- Some injustices may never be righted.

- The sin committed against you could go unconfessed to the grave!

But for the sake of the future, you can still say, "I'll put past hurts and fears aside. I want to hear again the call of my King. With Christ it's never too late to dream."

I want your story to be like the story of Hero in the tale I've been sharing.

"Now," said Mercie beside him, "the Rites of Adoption." The beautiful woman pressed two fingers to Hero's forehead. She steadied the back of his head with her other hand. The Rangers in the near circle lifted their hatchets, blades pointed toward him, and a hum, one note only, began.

"I, wife of Caretaker, war-maiden Ranger, do implant you, Ranger Hero, with this proof of parentage. You will always know you belong to us. You are ours. Orphan no more, you are heir to all we hold."

Hero closed his eyes and listened to the simple one-note hum. The place on his forehead which Mercie touched grew warm; then the gentle warmth diffused through his whole body. It was only when he opened his eyes that he realized every hatchet had been sheathed and that the hum he heard, the one-note hum, was now in his own brain, in his own ears, in his own heart.

The people of Great Park began to leave; wordlessly, they withdrew into Deepest Forest. Amanda gave him a shy hug. Her eyes glistened with tears. On the edge of the crowd, special friends waved silent farewells. Each Ranger clasped his hand and then departed. The Sacred Flames dimmed and died, leaving only glowing charcoals to mark the circle.

Hero stood alone with Caretaker and old Mercie.

"It is time," said Caretaker. "We will accompany you as far as Burning Place."

So the three walked together out of Inmost Circle, through Deepest Forest, past the practice field, deserted in the night, along the path by Caretaker's cottage where the latest outcasts rested in sleep, down the edge of Wildflower Woods to the old stone gates of Great Park.

A faint melon-wedge of light cracked the night sky, and Hero realized he would leave Great Park at the same time of day, dawn, that he had once entered it so many seasons ago.

Caretaker raised his hatchet and the familiar hymn-hum began. The gates creaked open slowly, and the three walked beneath the inscription: WELCOME ALL WHO HUNT.

Hero turned and watched the gates close behind him. "Will I ever see this place again?" he wondered out loud.

Mercie pulled him around to face Enchanted City. "Nonsense," she snapped. "You'll see it every time you close your eyes." Little as she was, she was now without pity and her grasp was mighty on his arm.

The two old people walked on either side of the boy. Hero dragged his heavy feet through the garbage dump, filled with rotten refuse, which separated Great Park from Enchanted City. Closer they came, closer and closer to Burning Place, just outside the city walls. And all the while, Hero sensed that Mercie and Caretaker were growing fainter, dimming somehow here in the rank air that smelled of smoke and fire. They were fading away from him. In this soft light, Hero read a sign which proclaimed:

THERE IS NO SUCH THING AS A KING.
DEATH TO PRETENDERS!

His feet kicked the soft ashes, and Hero knew he had finally returned, come back to the one place that he hated above all others.

"Mercie," he whispered. "Caretaker?"

They were gone.

29

They had left him here on the edge of Burning Place, alone, without aid. Abandoned. Helpless. Unloved. No, no wait. Hero took a deep breath.

He closed his eyes and thought back to where he had just been. Inmost Circle. Within the leaping Sacred Flames. He remembered the cry, "To vows!" and recalled the strong pulse of life clasped in the Ranger grasp. He was not alone. He might be on the edge of the evil Enchanted City, but wonderful things had happened to him. He belonged to somebody. He was loved.

At that moment, with his eyes still closed, he heard the lovely hum. It was not just a memory out of the past. It was with him now, in his ears, in his own brain. As Hero listened, the flailing in his heart was quieted. The hum grew from one note to many, and from many notes to the full music of Great Celebration.

And there in the light of dawn, of a new day, as the people of the city ended their work and prepared to sleep, Hero lifted his head and held forth his arms. His back straightened, Ranger tall, and he began the dance, kicking the ashes of Burning Place as he stepped to the glorious chords of the inward melody. And for those who were still awake to hear, a laugh, young and joyous, rose from outside the walls and settled in the morning air.

For the lad, Hero, discovered that when one belongs to the Kingdom, he is never alone in the terrible places of the world; he can always hear the single, clear-note hum.

FOR DISCUSSION AND REFLECTION

1. Have you recently heard someone in a conversation give evidence of holding on to a painful past experience? How common a problem do you think this is?

2. Why do painful past experiences often inhibit people from dreaming God's dreams for themselves or for the church?

3. Almost everyone has had a negative church experience of one kind or another. What is a memory like this you might do well to put behind you?

4. Do you, like Gideon, have any fears of moving forward to accomplish God's dreams for you? What healing needs to be accomplished in this area?

5. If a person said, "I don't know how to put memories and fears like this behind me," what advice would you offer?

6. How good does "daring to dream again" sound to you?

Readings

I doubt we can ever put our pasts *behind* us when we've never put them *before* us. Yet many of us stall on the starting line of change because we fear that we'll lose family members' approval and affection.

I once counseled with a charming thirty-something Christian who grew up in a subtly, but profoundly, unhealthy home. She said her birth family's motto was "family first." I think that meant, "Ignore and don't talk about who and what's hurtful in this family." An alternative translation might be: "Don't rock the boat (with truth) even if it's the Titanic!"

We will never begin the move from hurting to healing until we answer the question: "Whose rules rule?" The person whose rules we are living by is god to us! If, in an attempt to gain the parental seal of approval, we continue to live by the rules of hurting, hurtful parents, we will continue our hurting, hurtful ways. But if we choose to know God and put him on the throne of our lives, we will begin to live by his rules. And, as we've already seen, God takes truth very seriously.

I read somewhere that calling a thing by its correct name is the beginning of change. Some of us will need to begin calling our family loyalty *lying,* if that is its correct name. Yet, just contemplating such a genuinely truth-based approach to our entire lives, we may feel as alien in our families as salmon would be in the Sahara! Yet God and commitment to change call us to begin dealing honestly with our pasts as well as our present lives. We must face the pain inherent in becoming truth-tellers in truth-fearing families. We are foolish to expect reality-phobic family members to jump up, click their heels together, and exclaim, "Oh, good goody. We've all been wondering when someone would get healthy enough to start changing so that we'd be confronted with our personal and family dysfunction and be dragged kicking and screaming into greater wholeness!" It just doesn't work that way.

In unhealthy systems, whether they're families or companies, the person who sees and speaks the problem becomes the problem. Instead of working to resolve the problem, such systems focus on removing the problem-perceiver.

Hurt People Hurt People,
Sandra D. Wilson, Thomas Nelson, pages 94–95.

•••

Through fifteen years, as tapes have gone out all over the world, letters and testimonies have confirmed my belief that there is another realm of problems which requires a special kind of prayer and a deeper level of healing by the Spirit. Somewhere between our sins, on the one hand, and our sicknesses, on the other, lies an area the Scripture calls "infirmities."

We can explain this by an illustration from nature. If you visit the far West, you will see those beautiful giant sequoia and redwood trees. In most of the parks the naturalists can show you a cross section of a great tree they have cut, and point out that the rings of the tree reveal the developmental history, year by year. Here's a ring that represents a year when there was a terrible drought. Here are a couple of rings from years when there was too much rain. Here's where the tree was struck by lightning. Here are some normal years of growth. This ring shows a forest fire that almost destroyed the tree. Here's another of savage blight and disease. All of this lies embedded in the heart of the tree, representing the autobiography of its growth.

And that's the way it is with us. Just a few minutes beneath the protective bark, the concealing, protective mask, are the recorded rings of our lives.

There are scars of ancient, painful hurts . . . as when a little boy rushed downstairs one Christmas dawn and discovered in his Christmas stocking a dirty old rock, put there to punish him for some trivial boyhood naughtiness. This scar has eaten away at him, causing all kinds of interpersonal difficulties.

Here is the discoloration of a tragic stain that muddied all of life . . . as years ago behind the barn, or in the haystack, or out in the woods, a big brother took a little sister and introduced her into the mysteries—no, the miseries of sex.

And here we see the pressure of a painful, repressed memory . . . of running after an alcoholic father who was about to kill the mother, and then of rushing for the butcher knife. Such scars have been buried in pain for so long that they are causing hurt and rage that are inexplicable. And these scars are not touched by conversion and sanctifying grace, or by the ordinary benefits of prayer.

In the rings of our thoughts and emotions, the record is there; the memories are recorded, and all are alive. And they directly and deeply affect our concepts, our feelings, our relationships. They affect the way we look at life and God, at others and ourselves.

We preachers have often giving people the mistaken idea that the new birth and being "filled with the Spirit" are going to automatically take care of these emotional hang-ups. But this just isn't true. A great crisis experience of Jesus Christ, as important and eternally valuable as this is, is not a shortcut to emotional health. It is not a quickie cure for personality problems.

Healing for Damaged Emotions,
David Seamands, Victor Books, pages 11–12.

Chapter Two
Discover God's Present Involvement in Your Life

God's dreams for us seldom unfold as quickly as we would like. That's frustrating, but the experience is not uncommon.

Do you remember the account in Scripture of young David being brought home from watching the flocks? Samuel was attempting to discover which one of Jesse's boys had been chosen by the Lord to replace Saul as king. Having looked over all the candidates presented to him, the prophet still had no positive word from the Lord. "Are these all the sons you have?" he asked.

"There is still the youngest," Jesse answered, "but he is tending the sheep." His comment implied that David was hardly of age to be a serious possibility. But when David got home, the Lord told Samuel, "Rise and anoint him; he is the one" (see 1 Samuel 16:1–13).

So God himself said through his prophet that David was to be the next king. But many years would pass, involving any number of hair-raising escapades, before David would finally sit on Israel's throne. God's promise didn't come true immediately. In the meantime, I'm sure this former shepherd boy had frequent reason to doubt that the Lord's dream for him would ever be realized.

Here, then, is another barrier to seeing God's dreams validated in our lives. It's the inability to recognize his involvement in our everyday world and, therefore, giving up too soon on is long-range promises.

In the book *Tales of the Resistance*, Scarboy doesn't become a hero overnight, either. But, like David, he truly is a hero. The question is whether or not he can hold on to what his King has promised, even if it isn't quickly realized. Scarboy's first battle in Enchanted City isn't with a giant like Goliath; nevertheless his bravery is put to the test.

> *Din . . . din . . . din . . .* The death drums were sounding another beat, faster and faster—a battle beat. Hero realized that more Burners and Breakers were gathering in striking formation. He had done a foolhardy thing. Even with the hatchet in hand, he was only one against many. He was in the middle of the Enchanter's territory, with no fellow Ranger to come to his aid. His only chance was in taking his opponents by surprise.
>
> Rushing down the stairs, Hero swung into the battle tactic he had learned in the War of Fire in Great Park. "To the King! To the Restoration!" he cried, holding his hatchet with both hands. He jumped into the middle of the band of captured orphans. "Scatter!" he shouted. "Take off your blindfolds and run!"
>
> With his weapon at arm's length, Hero began to whirl as the children scattered, climbing stairs,

turning street corners, scurrying into holes. Round and round Hero whirled, cutting a circle of emptiness between himself and his would-be captors.

The Enchanter's men were so intent on taking him prisoner, they let the children escape. For a moment, Hero felt a defiant gladness.

S-C-A-R-B-O-Y! S-C-A-R-B-O-Y!

The Enchanter's evil eye had spotted him. The moment his old name was shouted, Hero began to freeze. His feet were leaden; the hatchet felt so heavy. Closer and closer inched the Burners and Breakers. One of the Breakers caught Hero's eye and held it with a stare; then he lifted his ugly cudgel over his head.

HARNK-HARNK! HARNK-HARNK! From opposite directions two taxicabs came careening down the narrow alley, their horns blaring, their speed frightening. *HARNK-HARNK!*

The Enchanter's men scattered, and the taxis screeched to a stop within inches of the stunned Hero.

"Need a ride, buddy?" A burly arm grabbed Hero and pulled him roughly into the front seat. As Hero frantically yanked the door shut behind him, his cab blasted into reverse and squealed around another corner. Within seconds a whole fleet of taxis raced out of alleys and side streets. They drove for a while in a straight line, and then veered off in opposite directions. *HARNK! HARNK! HARNK!* Their horns blared in great commotion, and for a moment Hero felt safe. No pursuer would know which cab had kidnapped him.

But was he under arrest or under protection?

Hero could just read the signs over the huge garage before the overhead door thudded shut behind them: City Taxi Company. There was a hustle as the driver detached from the power source. Hero's door was yanked open and he was pulled out.

"Ey, bub. Big Operator wants to see you in the terminal office." The cabbie jerked his head to the left, and then drove off. A man in uniform motioned Hero toward a glassed-in office. . . .

The next thing he knew, his wrist was being clasped in the Ranger way. "Well, son. Most Rangers infiltrate Enchanted City as subtly as possible. The whole town knows you've arrived, not to mention the powers that be in the Dagoda. But welcome to the Resistance. We are all King's men and women here, working for the Restoration."

Hero's mouth dropped, and Big Operator smiled.

"Yessir, the dispatchers had themselves a job getting you out of that tight spot. It's not easy moving a taxi vanguard into position on a moment's notice.

"By the way, I think we picked up most of the orphans. That scattering tactic was pretty effective. The Resistance can use a man like you. How would you like to see the rest of the operation?"

The two walked to the middle of the taxi terminal, a large underground cavern with a huge map of Enchanted City on one wall. Big Operator pointed to purple paper flags stuck all over the map. "Sightings," he explained. "The King has been sighted all over the city. The Enchanter's nervous. . . . Our informants say the Dagoda's been a hot place with a whole lot of fire flying." . . .

Hero's mind would not stop whirling. He didn't know which question to ask first. "But—but what

40

about the Enchanter? How do you get by with this
in the middle of Enchanted City?"

Big Operator smiled, but it was a grim expression.
He put his arm around the lad's shoulders. "Make no
mistake. The Enchanter is evil and he's dangerous—
never forget it. The closer the Restoration, the more
Sightings of the King—the more dangerous and des-
perate he will become." Then his smile became
almost cocky. "But the truth is, the Enchanter only
has power over those who fear him. Here in the Taxi
Resistance, we are subjects of the King.
Consequently, we are not afraid."

SIGHTINGS OF THE KING

There's something important here which, I believe,
applies to all of life. When "sightings" of the King begin
to multiply, our world starts to get exciting. How
thrilling to hear that the Monarch's presence has been
witnessed. God's bigger dreams quickly come into sharp-
er focus when we're reminded of his involvement in our
lives. When this happens, though, it's also true that the
enemy engages us in fiercer combat.

Even so, I say, "Good for you!" to those who have
trained themselves to recognize God in the everyday.
These are the men and women who find it easiest to sus-
tain their belief in God's long-range dreams. That's
because they see daily evidence that the Lord hasn't for-
saken them.

It was that way with David. One "God sighting"
occurred while, as a young refugee, he was hiding in a

41

cave with his band of so-called outlaws. They were being
tracked by King Saul and 3,000 chosen men. When the
king had to relieve himself, lo and behold, he did so in
the very cave where David was hiding. Then Saul decided to rest there awhile.

David's friends, far back in the cave, whispered that
the Lord had given his enemy into his hands! "This isn't
mere coincidence," they were saying in essence. "God's in
it." But the only thing David did was to creep up unno-
ticed and cut off a corner of Saul's robe. David knew
that in this incident God was saying, "I'm looking out
for you, David. See how I can give Saul into your hands
whenever I want!" (See 1 Samuel 24:1–4.)

There were numbers of situations like this in David's
life. This specific event involved unusual linkage and
timing. Of all the caves in that region, Saul chose the
very one in which David and his men were hiding. It
had to be more than chance that caused Saul to say,
"Stop! That cave over there is going to be my restroom
for the moment."

The point is, we all can maintain excitement about
God's larger dreams for us when we keep close track of
his involvement in our everyday world. Keeping close
track of his involvement is important. I do it as part of
my daily journaling. I've recorded thousands of such
entries in my lifetime. What faith-builders they are.

This exercise is truly one of the most pleasurable
aspects of my life. Seldom does a day go by when I don't
see an obvious answer to prayer, some unexpected

evidence of God's care, or maybe special help he provides to do his work in the world.

Possibly some of my "sightings" are coincidence, but I'm convinced that an awful lot of them aren't. And one way or the other, I choose to give God the credit.

In the Bible we see that this is what David did too! He recorded what happened to him and acknowledged it as God's work. Psalm 57 is an example of such an account. It's a song of David praising the Lord for His help "when he had fled from Saul into the cave." Read these verses and picture yourself in David's situation.

> Have mercy on me, O God, have mercy on me,
>   for in you my soul takes refuge.
> I will take refuge in the shadow of your wings
>   until the disaster has passed.
> I cry out to God Most High,
>   to God, who fulfills his purpose for me.
> He sends from heaven and saves me,
>   rebuking those who hotly pursue me;
>   God sends his love and his faithfulness.
>
> I am in the midst of lions;
>   I lie among ravenous beasts—
> men whose teeth are spears and arrows,
>   whose tongues are sharp swords.
> Be exalted, O God, above the heavens;
>   let your glory be over all the earth.
> They spread a net for my feet—
>   I was bowed down in distress.
> They dug a pit in my path—
>   but they have fallen into it themselves.

My heart is steadfast, O God,
  my heart is steadfast;
  I will sing and make music.
Awake, my soul!
  Awake, harp and lyre!
  I will awaken the dawn.

I will praise you, O Lord, among the nations;
  I will sing of you among the peoples.
For great is your love, reaching to the heavens;
  your faithfulness reaches to the skies.
Be exalted, O God, above the heavens;
  let your glory be over all the earth.

Hide-and-seek is a universal game. Everyone has played it at one time or another. In the Scriptures it's almost as if the Lord invites us to go on a spiritual hide-and-seek. "You will seek me and find me when you seek me with all your heart." That's Jeremiah writing on God's behalf to the exiles in Babylon. "'I will be found by you' declares the Lord" (Jeremiah 29:13–14). So even when his people are captives in another land, it's as if the Lord tells them, "Don't stop looking for me!"

The "fun factor" in looking for God comes out in a verse like Psalm 105:3, "Let the hearts of those who seek the Lord rejoice." And we do rejoice frequently when we see the Lord working in our lives.

"Seek and you will find." That's how Jesus issued the challenge in his Sermon on the Mount (Matthew 7:7). He was talking about the reality of his now-and-future kingship.

As I expressed earlier, one of the most pleasurable aspects of my own involvement in Christ's kingdom is writing down each day what I call my "God Hunt sightings." These are occasions when I see the Lord acting in my behalf in a special way, and I choose to attribute the events to him. In our family we've come up with four categories that help define what we're talking about.

ANSWERS TO PRAYER

One is an obvious answer to prayer. Let me illustrate. I hesitated to attend a conference because I needed to prepare a rather complicated paper for a particular man. It was due the day I was to get back. I went to the conference anyway and was overjoyed to see that this person was also there. When I checked in at the hotel desk, I was so surprised that I just said hello and walked on.

As soon as I got to my room I prayed, "Lord, I'm amazed this man is here. How wonderful it would be if we could talk for an hour or so and work through some of our concerns in person. But this is a huge conference. I may never run into him again. Please allow me to see him again—I'll immediately ask him if there's a time we can meet while we're here."

I unpacked my things, went down on the elevator to the main lobby, and saw this man coming in the front door of the hotel again. We talked briefly and set a time to get together the next morning. To me that was a marvelous God Hunt sighting. The time together helped me immensely.

This might not seem like a God Hunt sighting to you, but, as I've already explained, I choose to give the Lord the credit for what happens on these occasions. I admit some of my "sightings" may be coincidence, but I prefer to believe most of them aren't! And what matters is not whether I can convince someone else, but whether I'm satisfied that it's the Lord at work.

EVIDENCE OF HIS CARE

The second God Hunt category is unexpected evidence of his care.

I called from the office and asked my wife, Karen, "Where are you money-wise?" I needed to head home and pack. We were using some frequent flyer award tickets to take a couple of well-deserved days away. I had very little cash in the bank, although I figured we could use a credit card if need be. But maybe Karen had money.

Her answer was, "My bank account is as low as yours!"

"Just wondered," I responded. "See you soon."

In the next few moments an old friend stopped by the office and said, "Heard you and Karen were leaving for a few days. Knowing how you guys live, I thought you might need some cash. It's a gift; don't give it back. Have a good time. The Lord go with you."

Care of this sort is not an everyday occurrence. But I praise the Lord for friends and *also* for unexpected evidences like this of God's care.

UNUSUAL LINKAGE OR TIMING

A third God Hunt category is unusual linkage or timing, such as when David hid in the very cave Saul decided to rest in. It was too perfect to be mere chance.

Unusual linkage and timing is getting on an almost empty airplane and sitting across the aisle from someone who desperately wants to know about Jesus and how to personally meet him. God has provided an almost private setting and an hour-and-a-half flight during which you are able to lead the person to the Cross.

HELP TO DO HIS WORK

A last God Hunt category is what we call help to do his work in the world. It's having a new family attend the church with the very skills needed to replace those of a strong couple who have just moved out of town. It's having a friend call and share a story that works perfectly for the closing illustration in a Sunday school lesson you've been working on. It's saying, as David did, "I need a friend, Lord—a friend who's like a brother. This future kingship assignment you've given me isn't an easy one." And the Lord responds, "David, I've prepared the king's son, Jonathan, to be that friend to you."

Those God hunt categories, again, are:

1. An obvious answer to prayer
2. Unexpected evidence of his care
3. Any unusual linkage or timing
4. Help to do God's work in the world

47

Occasionally a God Hunt sighting will fit several categories. That's no problem. And sometimes a sighting is almost in a category of its own. Don't worry about that either.

What's important is the belief that the Lord is constantly calling to us, "Seek me. I'm here. I'm not that hard to find. Just look a little. Come on, now!"

Here's an important point. I believe it's necessary to write these sightings down. We need to keep a record of them. A list like this is great for reviewing when the dark days come. I make God Hunt sightings a regular part of my prayer journal.

To go on the God Hunt you may need to think in a new way. Some will have to learn to become like a child again, to renew that sense of wonder and delight. Others will need to break through a glass ceiling. Maybe you're not young like David was. That doesn't matter. It's never too late to start something good.

Beware when you no longer sense the joy of the daily God Hunt. What happens then is that we become secular, just like the world. To be secular means that we restrict the sacred life to an hour or two on Sunday morning, seldom seeing the supernatural interface with our everyday world. What a sad way to live . . . as secular Christians!

Let me return to *Tales of the Resistance.*

> Big Operator gave the lad with the scar an unlikely assignment: Keeper of the Chronicle of Sightings of the King. The chief of the Taxi Resistance knew

that those who look harder for what they seek often find more than they expect.

On-street sightings!" shouted Hero. "But—but I'm terrible at Sightings! I could hardly find the King in disguise in Great Park! How am I going to find him here in Enchanted City?" . . . "But what about my scar? All of the Enchanter's men have a description of me by now. You yourself said there was a manhunt."

Big Operator was not to be moved. "I need an operator with street savvy and Ranger training. It's imperative that someone keep records of the King's activities. Hide your scar. Stay away from lights. The weather's turning cool; wear a scarf. Of course, this is a dangerous assignment. If you're afraid . . ."

Hero started to say that it wasn't fear, but at that moment the buzzer in the terminal sounded the yellow alert, indicating that a taxi was approaching in haste. A mechanic began to crank up the great garage door. At the same moment, a dispatcher at the control panel shouted, "Sighting!" The King had made himself known somewhere in the city. With amazement, Hero and Big Operator watched two frightened children climb confusedly out of the back of the cab. The door slammed; an echo reverberated.

"Hey!" shouted the driver. "I left the King t'bring dese kids in—but the Enchanter's car's comin'! Better get back to action." The cabbie indicated the location of the Sighting to a monitor, "Heraldry post 101; Moire Oxan." A pin was immediately stuck in the map of Enchanted City.

"Wait a minute!" cried Big Operator, turning to the lad. "What do you say, Hero? I need a chronicler right now out on the street. Do you want to see the

King in action? The taxi can take you back."

To see the King—at that moment Hero forgot all his doubts. He clasped Big Operator's wrist in the Ranger way, grabbed his bag, and hurried to hop into the front seat of the taxi.

Amanda turned from the control board, shoved back her headset and earphones, and called, "Where are you going?"

Hero slammed the taxi door shut. The cabbie gunned the motor as the mechanic began to crank up the great door again. Hero leaned out the window and grinned. "To the streets. I'm going to see the King!"

There's a lot more to this part of the tale than I've shared, but it ends this way . . .

> *So Hero became the Keeper of the Chronicle of Sightings of the King. He was often in dangerous places, often filled with doubt; but he found more reason to believe than not to believe and he discovered for himself that in the Kingdom, where the King rules, believing is seeing.*

That's what I want for you. I want you to learn that seeing—having to have everything proved so that no one could possibly doubt—isn't believing. But often believing is seeing as we learn to interpret what happens with eyes of faith, experience the joy of sighting the hand of God in our everyday, become like children spiritually, accept God's invitation to play hide-and-seek, and become skilled at God Hunt sightings, not missing a thing.

And because we keep track of his involvement in our daily lives, we're excited to believe God's longer-range dreams for us will come true as well!

For Discussion and Reflection

1. When is it that God seems most removed from your everyday world?

2. Who is a person you feel experiences the presence of the Lord in an unusual way? Why do you think this is so?

3. As you look back on your life, what is a God Hunt sighting you recall?

4. What do you like most about going on a daily God Hunt?

5. Is there anything about going on a daily God Hunt that seems intimidating? What?

6. Talk about a time you believe God put a long-range spiritual dream in your heart.

READINGS

Out of Billings the travel agent had me booked on a trunk airline flight north, and so I went to the desk to check in.

"Sorry, sir," the agent said, "but that flight's canceled for today."

"When's the next flight?" I asked.

"Not till seven tomorrow morning."

"But I've got to get there. I have a speaking engagement tonight."

"Sorry, sir."

I stepped away from the counter and silently thanked God for this disappointment, asking Him to show me the reason for it.

Just then another man stepped up to the counter, a big, burly character who, when he learned of the canceled flight, let out with an air-blueing stream of profanity.

"Look," he bellowed, "you get me on a flight! I'm gonna lose a lotta money if I don't get up there!"

"I'm sorry," the agent said meekly. "There's nothing I can do."

A third man came to check in for the flight. He too displayed his temper, though not so vociferously as the first.

I stepped up to the two men. "Since there are three of us," I said, "why don't we charter a plane?"

"Good idea!" the big fellow exclaimed. Turning to the agent he said, "Get us some information right away on charter flights!"

In a few minutes we were out beside a small plane. The big fellow sat up front with the pilot, we two smaller men in the back.

"My name is Malcom Randall," my companion introduced himself.

"I'm Stanley Tam," I said. "What's your business?"

"I work for the government. You?"

"I'm from Lima, Ohio. We reclaim and refine silver and also have a plastics sales organization."

"You're here on business?"

"I'm speaking at a church tonight, telling about my experiences as a Christian businessman."

"That's fascinating. I wish I could hear you, but I'll be tied up with appointments."

"Would you let me share some of my experiences with you now?"

"Sure, why not?"

So I began my story.

"Say," he interrupted, "I've heard you speak! It was at a service club or something."

His sudden outburst threw me off for a moment.

"Well, how about that?" I said.

"Yeah, I sure have." He pointed to a pin on his lapel. "It was at a Lion's Club meeting somewhere. I'm out of town a lot, but I always try to get to the local club wherever I happen to be. Isn't that something?"

It so intrigued him to have run across me before, I had difficulty getting back on course.

But finally he said, "Go ahead. Finish the story."

As I continued, he grew more intensely attentive. I could see evidence of spiritual concern creep across his countenance.

"You know," he said when I had concluded my testimony, "almost every night I get down on my knees and try to pray. I confess my sins."

"Do you have God's peace in your heart?" I asked.

He shook his head. "That's something I know nothing about," he said.

"May I tell you how to find this peace?" I asked.

He nodded.

Moments later there on the plane God honored me with the privilege of bringing another man to a personal knowledge of His Son.

"You know something," this man said to me, "It was no accident the plane was canceled out of Billings. It was an act of God. He knew I needed to meet you!"

God Owns My Business,
Stanley Tam, Horizon House, pages 143–44.

•••

On the Saturday before the crucial congregational meetings, John Maxwell and his 100 prayer partners went out to what they believed would be the future site of Skyline Wesleyan. The more they prayed, the more they began getting a strange feeling, first individually, then in groups. After unimaginable agonizing, they began to admit to each other that collectively they were hearing God say, "This is not your site!"

At the congregational meeting the next evening, John rehearsed the process they had gone through to decide to purchase the property. It had seemed right from the business point of view, from the financial point of view, from the church management point of view, and from advice they had received from many sources. But one thing could outweigh all those positive indications—the word from the Lord received through earnest and effective prayer.

Even though Maxwell knew that many would be disappointed, he had built up enough faith in the hand of God working in his life and the life of the church through his prayer partners that he became bold. He recommended that Skyline Wesleyan Church withdraw the offer for the property. He also assured the congregation that if God was really telling them not to buy this property, it was because He had something much better in store for them. How much better no one could have imagined at the time!

The search process began once again. They located a beautiful 80-acre property and asked the owners twice if they would sell, but they were turned down both times. The prayer partners and others continued to pray. Soon a financial crunch came and the owners seemed more disposed to sell. Skyline made a very low bid of $1.8 million for the 80 acres, and the owners by then were in such a tight situation they reluctantly said they would sell. But the owners insisted on some fine print: If Skyline could not get the land zoned for a church, they would agree not to sell the land but would return the land and also pay the owners interest on the amount Skyline had spent.

The church, cognizant of the risk, closed the deal only to find out through an independent appraiser that the true value of the land was $4.5 million. Skyline Church had taken an even greater risk than they thought!

The church was also forced to buy three times the number of shares of water rights than necessary, and they paid $120,000 for them. But drought set in on Southern California, the value of the water rights soared, and the owners begged them to sell two-thirds of the rights back. By that time the two-thirds were worth $250,000 and as part of the deal, the church persuaded the former owners to rescind the clause that they would have to give back the property if it were not zoned for their use. So God gave them the property for the price they had offered with no fine print, along with an extra $130,000!

But that is not all. They had the "80-acres" surveyed and found that the land was really 110 acres! Then the Water District needed 10 acres on the low part of the land and offered to trade 30 acres at the top, right where John Maxwell had envisioned the parking lot, for the 10. They now had 130 acres. Finally they were offered $4 million for a stretch of industrially-zoned land, which they did not need for the church anyway.

Skyline Wesleyan now has a lovely church site, probably worth more than $10 million, for which they ended up not paying a thing!

This was all because of prayer. Through prayer, the pastor's prayer partners had heard God say, No. Their spiritual maturity caused them to be bold enough to follow what they knew would be an unpopular course of action. Once they followed, they began hearing a series of yesses from God that carried them, their pastors, the church board, and the congregation over the threshold and into the greatest era of Skyline Wesleyan's history.

Prayer Shield,
C. Peter Wagner, Regal, pages 21–23.

Chapter Three
Establish Godly
Goals for
Your Future

A lot of people daydream about someday striking it rich. They fantasize about how they'll spend their millions. Keeping that dream alive must be important, because some would-be millionaires actually gamble with their hard-earned money.

As an adult, for me the odds of winning a state lottery seem infinitesimally small. So I'm not tempted to save my money for a "glamorous, fun-filled visit" to a gambling casino. I don't care if it's run by the Mafia or the government; count me out.

But back when I was in upper elementary school, a carnival came to our area in southern Illinois. The traveling company set up its wares in the big field at 30th and Main on the east edge of town. Our house was on 27th, just a couple of blocks away, so we neighborhood kids got to witness everything firsthand.

The giant Ferris wheel was the first attraction to go up. It was awesome. Then the tents and concession stands began to form a midway. Last, a huge net was hung on supports. It was designed to catch "Zaccheeni, the human cannonball." Each night he was shot from what looked like a cannon mounted on the back of a big flatbed truck. Because his flight path took him up over the Ferris wheel, I'm told almost everyone waited around to see what would happen.

The carnival officially opened on a Friday night, and I recall as a boy being in bed and hearing the music over the loud speakers. My folks said we could go during the day but not in the evening. So early the next morning I rendezvoused with friends, and we were off to see the wonders.

STEP RIGHT UP!

The tilt-a-whirl and the sword swallower and the shooting gallery caught the attention of my friends. But what I was fascinated by was a booth that featured what looked like miniature steam shovels. For a quarter a try you operated knobs that would make the claw (or the shovel) go up, down, and sideways; and open and close. Wonderful prizes were there to be picked up by this little shovel, including—would you believe—a roll of five dollars' worth of quarters. I watched a man win one of those rolls!

I saw others try and fail. But after a while I figured out what they were doing wrong. So eventually I just had to try my hand at it.

The test turned out to be harder than I had thought. And before I knew it, my only dollar was gone. However, on the last try I almost captured that elusive stack of quarters.

Now it was decision time. Back at home I had five dollars in my top dresser drawer. I was saving that to buy a new trick at Harry's Magic Shop. But with what I had already learned about the miniature steam shovels, I knew that in just another turn or two I could capture those quarters. Then I'd have my five dollars back, the dollar I had already lost, plus at least three or four dollars I wouldn't even have to spend.

I don't have to finish the story.

What was it that would prompt a boy to lose every cent he had on that stupid game? In the end I had absolutely nothing to show for my carnival experience— no hot dog, no pop, no ride on the octopus, nothing! I couldn't even tell my folks I'd had a great time.

Maybe it was the dream that I could get around the tough things all boys had to do to get "rich"—mow lawns, deliver papers, hawk ice cream at ball games. I don't know. But I do know that most days for most people are horribly routine, and life tends to go by rather quickly. All of that makes us susceptible to whatever appears a bit more exciting and bigger than life.

TRAGIC DECISIONS

There must have been a bit of a carnival atmosphere to traveling with Jesus. Certainly he drew great crowds. I wonder what the odds were that the Son of God would choose as one of his disciples a man who found money a bigger attraction than ministry. This member of the Twelve was supposedly laying up for himself treasures in heaven by being a part of Jesus' traveling entourage. But insiders testified that this disciple also worked at doing all right by himself here on earth as well!

Am I being too hard on Judas? I don't believe so.

Listen to these observations from his fellow disciple, John. Remember the story in John 12 of Mary taking a pint of expensive perfume and pouring it on Jesus' feet? It was Judas who objected, asking, "Why wasn't this perfume sold and the money given to the poor?" (v. 5).

Here's John's contention (v. 6): "[Judas] did not say this because he cared about the poor but because he was a thief." That's a strong accusation, isn't it? Observe what John writes next: "As keeper of the money bag, [Judas] used to help himself to what was put into it." Wow!

I have to assume that John is being truthful here. He reports that when Judas wanted to, he stole from the group's kitty. What this information reveals is that, at the very least, Judas's love of money was a strong enough urge that he was willing to steal.

We also know that for money—thirty pieces of silver—Judas was willing to turn informant.

Maybe that urge to be rich was there from the beginning. My suspicion is that initially Judas was captured by the person of Christ and his message about his kingdom, or kingship. Then when the miracles started happening and the crowds began to swell, Judas knew he was in on the ground floor of something unique. When a movement expands and experiences momentum like this, there is always the possibility of financial growth that can be exploited, which apparently is what Judas did.

But as months passed, and years, and the time eventually came for that final entry of the team into Jerusalem, Judas was quite aware that Jesus wasn't performing the way he felt their leader should. Christ wasn't taking advantage of "the messianic moment."

Realizing the kingdom wasn't going to be established the way he thought (i.e., a kingdom where he would have a prominent place), maybe this disciple felt he could best profit by disclosing the whereabouts of Christ to his enemies. Avarice would be a key motivation for Judas. That was, of course, a tragic decision.

When did the relationship between Judas and Jesus first begin to unravel? Was it back when Jesus said, "No one can serve two masters"? The two masters Christ named specifically were God and Money. We can't be sure when Judas first became disillusioned.

But in broad strokes, Judas's problem was that somewhere along the line his self-centered dreams took priority over Jesus' kingdom dream. How often that has happened with people who have followed Christ. Like Judas, they start thinking about money more than ministry.

Judas is an exception in the sense that he had the opportunity to spend so much time with Jesus. Certainly he should have figured out that in a relationship with Christ, when one gives priority to self-centered dreams it's not a win-win situation.

But Judas appears to be more the rule than the exception when we ask whether his attitude is a common one. The Jerusalem crowd had done the same thing earlier that week. They welcomed Christ into their city yelling, "Hosanna," a Hebrew expression meaning "save us now." Restated, "Deliver us from our oppressors and we'll buy into your kingship, Jesus. We want you to be the promised Messiah. 'Blessed is he who comes in the name of the Lord!'"

Again, here were self-centered dreams taking priority over what God had in mind for his Son to do. Therefore, this would not have been a double win situation.

It's a win-win relationship when we learn to make God's dreams for us our dreams as well. Obviously it's a win for God because then we are his faithful servants. But it's also a win for us because we have a marvelous Lord who cares deeply about the well-being of his loyal subjects.

But we never want to forget that he is Lord and we are his servants. That's what Paul wrote in 1 Corinthians 4:1–2. "So then, men ought to regard us as servants of Christ and as those entrusted with the secret things of God. Now it is required that those who have been given a trust must prove faithful." Paul did this, but Judas did not.

One man started well and ended poorly. The other got off to a terrible start but eventually came on very strong. In God's kindness he didn't say to Paul that it was too late for him to buy into Christ's kingship dream. The faithful servant is the one who takes great delight in the dreams of his or her master. And he or she is rewarded accordingly.

WORTH IT ALL

Throughout this book, I've been using sections from *Tales of the Resistance,* which my wife, Karen, and I wrote. In *Tales of the Resistance,* Big Operator, the head of the Resistance in Enchanted City, exemplifies the wonderful delight a subject takes in helping fulfill his King's dreams. Let me share a short section from near the end of the book. The chapter's called, "The Orphan Exodus," and it will be referenced once again when you get to chapter 6 of this book. Big Operator and his King have pulled off a daring rescue of many orphan children.

Big Operator stood now at the street entrance to the pavilion; the beastly wolves lay silent in a stupor of sleep. He put two fingers to his mouth and blew a cabbie signal. At this, his master strategy went into operation. The first taxi accelerated to curbside, the first ready orphan group climbed into the back and front seats. The driver honked and then hurried off toward the garbage dump as another cab pulled up to take another load, followed by another and another.

And inside the King continued to speak the children's names, and with each naming the Orphan Keeper grew grayer, more haggard, leaking hot air. Her hair lost its luster, her teeth grew black and straggly until all could see her for her true self: a wicked hag who had gorged on the energy and youth and beauty of the children given to her keeping, a faker whose evil power was not her own, a no-people in disguise, as were all who gave themselves to do the will of the Enchanter. Finally she was nothing but a pile of dust covered by filthy red and purple rags, her gold melted and her jewels turned to powder.

And Big Operator was glad; his heart leaped with gladness. He knew the Enchanter would take revenge, but if this be his last strategic rescue design ever, he had been at the side of his King as together they emptied the pavilion of every last orphan. He closed his eyes and listened to the taxi vanguard, *his* taxi vanguard, honking throughout all of Enchanted City. HARNK! HARNK!—here, there, and everywhere—HARNK! HARNK! It sounded in his ears like a raucous chorus of jubilant rescue.

The King stood beside him ready to leave and to accompany the escapees into Great Park. The handclasp between them was firm and long. Their anger was gone but, strangely, there was no exultation, just a quiet sadness. Both knew what dire consequences their defiant acts would set into motion. "Farewell," said the King, and they embraced, the embrace of two mighty men. The orphan exodus was accomplished.

Big Operator watched the King disappear into the night. And though he knew it was just his imagination, it seemed as though a crowd of children stood all over the city, clapping their hands and shouting "Bravo!" And when the last taxi had hurried away with the last load, on a whim Big Operator bowed to the city—and the applause rose louder in his heart.

For Big Operator had learned through the years of masterminding the taxi resistance that mighty deeds demand mighty risks, but that it is worth risking all for the sake of the Kingdom and the King.

It's worth the risk!

To think this way is not easy. But all things being equal, making Christ your Ruler results in the best life you can have in the world! How's that for a glass-shattering idea?

So be careful what you make your ultimate dream. Don't end up snookered and broke and embarrassed. Remember that Christ has all eternity to reward you for whatever suffering you receive on his behalf.

THE RESTORATION IS NEAR!

Here's another short section from *Tales of the Resistance*. The evil Enchanter has taken his awful revenge on Big Operator and his taxi resistance. He's trying to find the King and destroy him as well. This is a conversation between two Resistance members, young Hero and Amanda.

Hero sighed. The Chronicle was almost current. The orphan exodus had been recorded and he had only to write about these recent terrible events. "I think I can remember everything Big Operator ever said to me." He leaned back in the chair and quoted the chief. "'This is an occupied city; we are in the midst of enemy territory.'

"He was a rough man, Amanda,—but, everyone in the City Taxi Company knew he was a man of the mind as well. It was the chief who collected the fragments of song and unwritten stories from the tale keepers for the Chronicle. Without them that history would be almost forgotten—the tales of the always young King who once ruled this city with a firm but

67

benevolent hand, of the Age of Rebellion when the Enchanter lured away the loyalty of the citizenry, of how the King went into exile vowing to return when time enough had passed for all to discover the folly of such a choice, and of how the fire wizard placed an enchantment over the city and ruled his subjects with the power of fire."

Hero paused, remembering. "My own mother must have been a tale keeper—keeping alive the old, true tales. I remember her words on her dying bed: 'There is a King, a real King!'"

Amanda felt tired and saddened. When would they ever be able to go back to the old ways of field and forest?

"You love him, don't you?" she said, smiling gently.

"Yes," said Hero. "He's a gruff old gizzard, but he's a genius, too. He'd been experimenting with daylight. 'The whole city's supposed to run on it!' he'd say. Solar panels. Storage cells. Sun batteries. He was getting us ready to live in the Restoration, to live at day and sleep at night, to harness the sun to do the work that slave labor does now."

Amanda quoted Big Operator: "Work in harmony with the world; not in disharmony with it!" She punched the air with her fist. This was a favorite City Taxi Company saying; they almost heard his rough voice again. The two smiled sadly at each other.

With that Hero leaned his elbows forward on the desk and his face in his hands. His voice was tight with grief. "He's dead, Amanda. I know it in my heart. I can only hope that he died quickly."

The two were silent. Amanda didn't protest, didn't work to evoke false hope. She had already seen this

68

terrible truth deep in her own heart. After a while she spoke, "Did anyone tell you what Big Operator's last words were when he was taken captive? You'll need it for the Chronicle."

Hero shook his bowed head, and she continued. "He had been badly beaten; three or four Breakers attacked him. Destruction was dismantling his life-work; but as they were dragging him away, he struggled to his feet and called out for all of us to hear above the din, 'The Restoration is near!' They knocked him senseless as he must have known they would. But, Hero, I keep hearing his cry, over and over— *'The Restoration is near!'*

"The Restoration is near"—believe me, that's a great truth to live by. Yes, our King's dream will know fulfillment.

Personal dreams related only to this life are never enough. They will always come up short. They don't span time and eternity. That's why, even as Christians, when we give priority to self-centered dreams, we lose.

Don't view Jesus' role in your life primarily as someone to help you get what you have in mind—be it wealth, health, a comfortable life, security, a ripe old age, recognition, or power. That approach is precarious at best. It's the path Judas followed. It's the servant thinking about the master, "I look at you as a means for me to reach the goals of *my* agenda." That's the reverse of the way it should be. Good servants don't think or act in that manner.

What does a trustworthy servant keep as foremost in his or her mind? The desires and dreams of the master.

In that context the good Master, the gracious Lord, the true King of the universe, will see to it that such a servant is treated better than the best. Again, it's a win-win relationship when we learn to make God's dreams for us our dreams as well.

Now there's a good gamble. I can almost hear the other eleven apostles saying, "Amen! Amen!"

FOR DISCUSSION AND REFLECTION

1. Think about someone you know who once walked close to the Lord but no longer does. Without naming the person, tell what you think happened.

2. Which is more likely—gradually drifting away from the Lord or turning away from him suddenly? Why?

3. Explain how a church that was once close to the Lord could begin giving priority to more self-centered dreams.

4. How closely do your personal dreams align with what you feel God would say his dreams are for you?

5. Share a personal "Big Operator event," a time of great satisfaction when you felt you brought your King great pleasure.

6. Give specific reasons why it is a win-win relationship when we make God's dreams for us our dreams as well.

Readings

After two years of college and the study of business theory nearly bored me to death, I returned to the family business prepared to follow in my father's footsteps. I loved the adrenaline of the marketplace. I was charged by the challenge—to do things a little more efficiently, to organize better, to maximize resources. And to make a ton of money. I knew where I was headed and what I wanted.

And then came a leading from the Holy Spirit. The director of a Christian camp I worked at during the summers pulled me off to the side and asked me a question that shook me to my foundations. "Bill, what are you doing with your life that will last forever?" The question haunted me. I began to realize that my whole existence was wrapped around the here and now. Everything I was doing was self-centered and temporary. That question stripped me naked, and I discovered that without the planes and boats and fast cars I had little to give my life meaning. As I continued to work at the produce company, I felt more and more restless. Finally, I decided I needed to serve the Lord more directly. I wanted to be on the front lines of the spiritual battle.

When I told my dad of my decision, he said, "Fine, Bill. Now turn in your credit cards and your keys to the plane, the boat, and the cars. And don't entertain any ideas of coming back.

I got a job in a shipping department of a Christian organization in the Chicagoland area. I made minimum wage. I was nineteen. I'll never forget the time my father flew in to visit me. I was standing between two middle-aged women, stuffing little plastic awards into cellophane wrappers. My dad looked at his son, for whom he had held such high hopes. Not one usually given to changing his mind, he took me to lunch and said, "You can get on that plane with me and come home." I told him no; I didn't want to miss the adventure. And I meant it!

Descending into Greatness,
Bill Hybels and Rob Wilkins, Zondervan, pages 206–07.

•••

Not many months after my conversion, having a leisure afternoon, I retired to my own chamber to spend it largely in communion with God. Well do I remember that occasion. How in the gladness of my heart I poured out my soul before God; and again and again confessing my grateful love to Him who had done everything for me—who had saved me when I had given up all hope and even desire for salvation—I besought Him to give me some work to do for Him, as an outlet for love and gratitude; some self-denying service, no matter what it might be, however trying or however trivial; something with which He would be pleased, and that I might do for Him who had done so much for me. Well do I remember, as in unreserved consecration I put myself,

my life, my friends, my all, upon the altar, the deep
solemnity that came over my soul with the assurance that
my offering was accepted. The presence of God became
unutterably real and blessed; and though but a child
under sixteen, I remember stretching myself on the
ground, and lying there silent before Him with unspeakable awe and unspeakable joy.

For what service I was accepted I knew not; but a deep
consciousness that I was no longer my own took posses-
sion of me, which has never been effaced. It has been a
very practical consciousness. Two or three years later
propositions of an unusually favorable nature were made
to me with regard to medical study, on the condition of
my becoming apprenticed to the medical man who was
my friend and teacher. But I felt I dared not accept any
binding engagement such as was suggested. I was not my
own to give myself away; for I knew not when or how
He whose alone I was, and for whose disposal I felt I
must ever keep myself free, might call for service.

Within a few months of this time of consecration the
impression was wrought into my soul that it was in
China the Lord wanted me. It seemed to me highly
probable that the work to which I was thus called might
cost my life; for China was not then open as it is now.
But few missionary societies had at that time workers in
China, and but few books on the subject of China missions were accessible to me. I learned, however, that the
Congregational minister of my native town possessed a
copy of Medhurst's *China*, and I called upon him to ask

a loan of the book. This he kindly granted, asking me why I wished to read it. I told him that God had called me to spend my life in missionary service in that land. "And how do you propose to go there?" he inquired. I answered that I did not at all know; that it seemed to me probable that I should need to do as the Twelve and the Seventy had done in Judea—go without purse, or scrip, relying on Him who had called me to supply all my need. Kindly placing his hand upon my shoulder, the minister replied, "Ah, my boy, as you grow older you will get wiser than that. Such an idea would do very well in the days when Christ Himself was on earth, but not now."

I have grown older since then, but not wiser. I am more than ever convinced that if we were to take the directions of our Master and the assurances He gave to His first disciples more fully as our guide, we should find them to be just as suited to our times as to those in which they were originally given.

To China with Love,
J. Hudson Taylor, Dimension, pages 14–16.

Chapter Four
Empower Everything You Do for God with Prayer

Do impossible dreams ever come true? The answer to that question is, yes they do! Especially they do if we involve God in what's taking place and don't just rely on our own resources.

Let me illustrate with stories of two persistent women and what God did for each of them. The key to their success, I believe, is this: There's always a better chance that an impossible dream will come true if the person involved shows why it is to God's advantage to help bring it about.

One of the stories comes from the Old Testament. This woman was in a bad home setting, in a bad religious setting, and she had a bad history of humiliation. Her name was Hannah. She was married to Elkanah, but unfortunately she wasn't this gentleman's only wife. The good news is that she was his favorite. The bad news is that she was barren. But it wasn't too late for her to dream.

The Scriptures report that year after year, Elkanah

went up from his town to worship and sacrifice to the Lord Almighty at Shiloh, where Hophni and Phinehas, the two sons of Eli, were priests of the Lord. We know these two guys were bad news. Hophni and Phinehas were wicked. The religious scandals we've known in our day are nothing compared to the shenanigans of these brothers.

The Bible declares they had no regard for the Lord. They were having sex with the women who served at the entrance to the Tent of Meeting, and in strong-arm fashion they were stealing all the meat they wanted from those who brought animals for sacrifice. As priests, these men totally disregarded the prescribed religious ceremonial rules.

YEAR OF THE MIRACLE

In God's providence, however (this is a marvelous God Hunt sighting), the "year of the miracle" for Hannah took place when Eli, the wicked priests' father, was serving. That meant someone with spiritual sensitivity would witness what was about to happen. First Samuel, chapter 1, reveals that Hannah was "in bitterness of soul." Her rival wife had provoked her until she wept and couldn't eat. This verbal abuse came because Hannah didn't seem to be able to have children. Verses 10–11 read:

> In bitterness of soul Hannah wept much and prayed to the Lord. And she made a vow, saying, "O Lord Almighty, if you will only look upon your ser-

vant's misery and remember me, and not forget your
servant but give her a son, then I will give him to the
Lord for all the days of his life."

It's precisely at this point that Hannah did something
special. Whether it was conscious or unconscious, I can't
say, but she allowed her desires to overlap the desires of
God. Frequently our praying is just for selfish ends. But,
praise the Lord, Hannah had stumbled onto something
when she made this vow.

At first Eli thought she was drunk. That's because her
agony was so great. But she sobbed, "Not so, my lord . .
. I am a woman who is deeply troubled. I have not been
drinking wine or beer; I was pouring out my soul to the
Lord. . . . I have been praying here out of my great
anguish and grief" (vv. 15–16).

To this, Eli prophetically responded, "Go in peace,
and may the God of Israel grant you what you have
asked of him" (v. 17). Verse 20 is where we see that the
impossible dream came true: "So in the course of time
Hannah conceived and gave birth to a son." The meaning of her son's name was "because I asked the Lord for
him." Hannah hadn't forgotten her divine bargain.
"Because I asked the Lord for him," put into a word, is
the name Samuel. And Samuel was to be a remarkable
person from the time he was a young lad all the way
through old age, always being faithful to his heavenly
Master.

Again, the secret revealed here is that Hannah had
taken her impossible request to the Lord, and in doing

79

so she had leveraged, if you will, how it would be to God's advantage to grant her petition.

Often, I believe, the impossible dreams we dream would really be of little advantage to God were he to respond in the way we ask. Think about some of the prayer requests you've heard (or offered) recently. How well do they reflect God's kingdom goals?

OVERLAPPING DESIRES

A second example of a woman who allowed her desires to overlap God's dreams is the fictional character Amanda. This story comes from *Tales of the Resistance*.

> At first, Amanda came to the courtyard simply because she needed a rest from the stress of traffic dispatching. Now she came because the plight of the girl drew her, a plight she didn't understand.
>
> One night a damp fog stinking of sludge smoke and burning garbage settled on the city. Amanda walked the dark streets, restless for clean air and the sun and a romp on spongy moss. She was not afraid to roam at night. Amanda was not afraid of anything, except her own dangerous stubbornness—a lesson hard learned in a terrible incident which had brought shame to herself, pain to all she loved, and disaster to the only place she would ever call home.
>
> She had loved a forbidden thing and had not been the same child since. A child with wild flowers in her hair, whose laughter constantly announced her presence, Amanda once had loved extravagantly, without question. Now she questioned all loves and was cautious about loving anything.

On this night Amanda slipped into the courtyard. The lanterns cast an eerie glimmer in the fog which oozed from the streets under the heavy outer doors. She stood beneath the balcony window, glad that the girl would not have to make many appearances on this frightful night.

The bell whispered—oh, dear, she had gazed too long. The girl appeared; Amanda was sorry to have disturbed her. "She's very beautiful," said a voice from the shadows behind her.

Amanda whirled around! Who was hiding in the courtyard?

"Don't be afraid—" the form moved away from the cloisters. Even in the damp fog, its motion was familiar. The voice was comforting, a well-known voice.

Her old impudence returned. "Have you nothing better to do than frighten unsuspecting maidens in dark streets? I thought you were supposed to be out chronicling Sightings." But Amanda was glad to see her old friend. Though she had heard much about his exploits, their paths had not crossed since that first day's encounter in the taxi terminal.

Hero spoke in a low voice. "The same old Amanda. Be careful what you say. Anyone (or anything) may be hiding in the shadows. This is a bastion of the Enchanter."

He lifted a lantern from its hook and carefully shone it in the corners. They were alone. The girl on the balcony had taken her bored silence inside.

He was taller than she remembered. By the light of the lantern she noticed that the planes and angles of his face had broadened, outgrowing the scar which had disfigured a boy's cheek. Now the old wound

81

gave him a rakish, elegant air. He had become handsome.

She wanted to protest, "I'm not the same old Amanda. I'm no longer just a play friend!" But she suspected he had grown so tall he would never notice that she had grown as well.

He pulled her to a bench, where they sat together. "Big Operator told me that you come here often." He spread his dark blue slicker around her shoulders to shelter her from the damp. Its color reminded her of the soft, rich homespun of Ranger cloaks, of flashing silver insignias, of courage and proud command and of the forest cry, "The Kingdom comes!"

"Amanda, you need to be careful roaming through Enchanted City. Great dangers lurk in every corner of every street."

Amanda stiffened. Her answer was also low. "I can take care of myself."

But Hero was in earnest. "In Great Park you are the amazing princess who used to outspit and outaim any contenders! But this is my territory. Innocence is dangerous in Enchanted City. Case in point: Don't ever come out on rainy nights without a covering, some sort of mackintosh. Even the air bodes ill; people die of nightailment. The health you take for granted in Great Park, the healing powers of Mercie are not natural to this place."

Amanda felt an old indignation rise—she was not a child—but just as suddenly it slipped away. She had learned all too well the folly of arrogance. She *had* been cold. She *was* glad for the warmth of his shared rain cloth. He was right, the paths and forest trails were her native terrain; but the hard paving stones of this dark place were his. Now she must learn from him.

82

The courtyard doors to the street creaked open. A form crept in and Amanda felt Hero tense beside her and grasp the handle of the hatchet beneath his slicker. A Breaker had entered the courtyard. Amanda's own heart quickened; she had once seen the chalky white face, the piercing eyes, the chilling grin, the cudgel raised to bash her as she lay in pain. *To the King,* she mentally intoned. *To the Restoration.* The bell whispered; the girl came to the balcony; the Breaker gazed and withdrew to the streets.

Hero murmured again, "She's so beautiful even the no-people come to look."

"But her eyes, her eyes—they're blank. There's no life in them."

"Of course," explained Hero. "She's the Forbidden Princess."

"The Forbidden Princess?" Amanda asked. They were out on the street now, walking back to the Taxi Company.

City wise, the young man told her the story of the beautiful girls gathered together every year to serve as temple keepers for the Enchanter. Chosen for their courage as well as for their beauty, a terrible initiation separated those who were worthy from those who were only fair. The novitiates spent a night in a room with severed bulls' heads. Those who didn't weep or whine were chosen to become princesses who spent the rest of their young lives allowing the curious to gaze on their faces, but forbidden to speak to any admirers.

"How awful!" said Amanda.

"That's not all. Eventually they become wives to the Enchanter. The children they bear are the Enchanter's elite guard, Burners and Breakers, the no-people. The Enchanter has had thousands of wives. Most of them shrivel and waste away—heart-sickness. His embrace is so terrible that even beauty and courage are not protection enough."

They stood talking before the overhead garage door of the City Taxi Company and waited for a cab to return rather than bother a mechanic. Sometimes, in the rain, the city was almost beautiful the way the lights danced on the wet stones. A taxi beeped its horn, the crank creaked inside, the door slid upwards.

"Amanda?" Hero placed a hand on her shoulder. "Don't go to the temple courtyard so often. It's dangerous. There's nothing you can do for the princess, and Big Operator says your work as a dispatcher is invaluable. Hundreds have been helped because of your quick gifts of seeing and aiming."

Amanda watched him stride off into the night, confident, his back broad. Nothing she could do! Nothing she could do! Then who would help the forlorn girl? But wait—wait, she had promised nothing. Hero had forgotten too much; *she* had once slayed a dragon singlehandedly in mortal combat. Hero's job was chronicling Sightings, who was to say her job wasn't the rescuing of forbidden princesses?

Amanda went back to the courtyard every night. She went at different times between control board duty, taking different alleys and streets, but she told no one because she was afraid they would forbid her—and Amanda had had enough pain from forbidden loves.

What would Mercie do in the city, with her powers confined by enchantment? she asked herself.

Each night when Amanda sat in the courtyard, she

silently spoke the names of the King. Whenever the Forbidden Princess came to the balcony, Amanda closed her eyes, took sure aim, and with her powerful gift of seeing, pointed the names right at the girl's heart.

His Majesty . . . my Sovereign Liege Lord . . . His Eminence . . . the Benevolent Potentate . . . His Supreme Holiness . . . the Lord Monsiegneur . . . His Most Royal Highness . . . the Monarch of All . . . the true King . . . to Him and to the Restoration of His Kingdom!

As Amanda did her lonely work, she watched for the slightest flicker of life in the eyes staring from the balcony, but there was nothing. Guilty memory taunted her—*forbidden love, forbidden love.* Crucial concentration came hard. Then one night as she sighted inwardly, she was sickened by seeing the evil eye of the Enchanter, searching, darting to and fro— and Amanda understood she was in peril. She knew she should end her vigils, but there—there! That very night, a tear dropped from the corner of the girl's eye. A sign of life! Amanda knew she had come again to love a thing dangerous to love.

So Amanda returned, hiding in the shadows of the cloisters, scarcely breathing lest she draw the ominous attention of the evil eye in the nearby Dagoda but aiming the Names from her heart to the heart of the girl standing on the balcony. At last, at last, the Forbidden Princess lifted her eyes as though wakening from a trance, and then turned her head toward the shadows as though peering for the silent speaker of the Names.

The girl had been awakened. The Names had done their life-giving work. Now, how to get her out before horror overtook them both? A plan! Slip into the courtyard, hide; then help the princess escape in the daylight, when the city was sleeping.

FIT FOR A KING

If impossible dreams are to come true, they require all the help we can get. If a task doesn't take much effort, it probably doesn't qualify as an impossible dream. What seemingly impossible dreams are you daring to dream?

Are you comfortable being around people who dream impossible dreams? I am. I enjoy hearing about grand schemes for making the world better. That's one reason Christ's kingdom, or kingship, message is so attractive to me. This world needs a righteous monarch who has both the wisdom to rule and the power to enforce his decisions. But it also needs someone marked by great love for all people. I believe Christ fills all these roles.

I'm happy to identify myself as one of his subjects, more than pleased to be involved in a small part of his marvelous now-and-future kingdom, and thrilled to tap into this incredible plan of his that gives such dignity and meaning and purpose to life. I also find there's enough room under his colossal umbrella to come up with challenging "impossible dreams" that are subpoints, or subdreams, of his.

When my dreams are consistent with Christ's dreams, I can expect his support in helping pull them off. The more my dreams overlap his, the more I can expect his aid when I need and request it.

Examine your dreams to see if there's a good reason to

believe that the Lord will help you. Will God really benefit in any way if your dreams come true, or are the plans
strictly of your own making and unrelated to what he's
about?

Amanda's impossible dream was to rescue the Forbidden
Princess from the hold of the Enchanter. Her unselfish
idea was to see this sad young woman come to know the
real King, and Amanda prayed for the princess, using his
names. Would the King be of any help? Would he answer
her prayers? Would he get involved in the rescue?

The next night Amanda left her earphones and
headset hanging neatly on their hook, finished her dispatcher's notes, and crept without telling anyone into
the little temple where she hid in the darkest corner.
Finally, the gatekeeper turned the key in the outside
lock. To her surprise she heard him say, *"She's locked
inside."*

Which she? Amanda wondered. Her breath quickened. Eyes shut, looking inward, she was horrified to
see the eye of the Enchanter looking straight at her!
An evil smile lit up his face. Closing off sight, she hurriedly began the litany of names. This time, she spoke
them aloud, urgently evoking the full sum of powers
available to her.

"His Majesty the King!" The Forbidden Princess
walked to the balcony. "My Sovereign Liege!" The girl
leaned over the wrought iron, as Amanda herself
walked boldly out of the shadows to the paving stones.
"His Eminence!" The eyes of the Forbidden Princess
filled with tears. "The Most Benevolent Potentate!"
The tears splashed on the stones. "His Supreme

87

Holiness!" The sky overhead began to shine slightly with a faint cast of dawn light. "The Lord Monsiegneur!"

The girl broke the silence and spoke, rather wept aloud hysterically, "It is too late—too late! Oh-oh-oh-oh! The Enchanter comes today to take me to the bridal chamber.

There was a pounding at the gate. BLAM! BLAM! BLAM! Amanda's heart failed. *Too late!* The distant echo of the death drums began to sound—*oom-bha-pah, oom-bha-pah*—calling sentries from the Dagoda to action.

What had she done? Awakened the princess out of her unfeeling numbness so she would be totally aware of the torture ahead? Placed her own valuable gifts of seeing and perfect aim as hostage to the enemy? These loves, these loves, these terrible loves! Would she never learn that love was dangerous? Why risk so much for one miserable girl among so many? Would she never learn about forbidden things?

The outer door—a key! Too late. The gatekeeper had returned.

Amanda drew herself to full stature and shouted the last names. "To the Monarch of All! To the King! To the Restoration of his Kingdom!" She knew she uttered treason and death was the penalty for her actions. But she was a princess of Great Park. Her heritage was of royal lineage; she would not whine or cry out or beg for mercy. For the sake of the King, she would march proudly to Burning Place.

Amanda held high her head as a man entered through the swinging gates.

He said, "Thank you, my sister. You honor me

well." It was the King himself!

Amanda gasped. "But how? The locked latch—the key—" Through the open gates she could hear the death drums beating louder, faster.

"Did you forget that I can open all closed doors?"

He looked very plain. There were no golden highlights in his hair, his clothes were common—but the voice! It sounded of clear waters falling over great boulders, of winds blowing across fragrant fields. And the eyes! They contained the hush of the deep far sky itself, vast and infinite.

"Let us hurry to finish this work you have begun," he said, and he stepped beneath the balcony where the princess was weeping hysterically with her head hidden in her arms. "Beloved!" he called quietly. "My beloved!"

The girl raised her head, and her eyes grew wide and her weeping stopped. The voice of the One of the Names had spoken; she knew him instantly and reached out her hands in an appeal for rescue. Clambering up the vines to the balcony, the King quickly lowered the princess by her wrists to the courtyard stones.

"We are a little short of princesses right now where I come from," he explained gently after he himself had vaulted down. "They're all growing up and accomplishing great things in the world—"

When your impossible dream is obviously going to advance the kingdom, you have every reason to believe that the King will give your dream his full attention. This is true even if he doesn't demonstrate his support until what appears to be the last possible moment.

DREAM POWER

When considering the dreams or aspirations we hold, prayer becomes an important topic to be knowledgeable about. You see, dreams of any magnitude will burn you out if you substitute busyness for spiritual empowerment.

Obviously no one would knowingly make that mistake. But what happens is that the workload takes on a life of its own. The demands of the schedule gradually increase. The pressures become more and more immediate. God sometimes seems far away, so we take matters into our own hands.

After a while, prayer, which appears to have a slow payoff, seems to fight with the "more urgent matters," important things that just have to get done. We think, *There's really nothing I can do to change that. Deadlines are deadlines.* Repeated days and weeks and months of pressure set us up in a pattern of racing around, and we think there's no longer enough time left for prayer. When that happens, the impossible dream becomes a monster and must be pulled back on course.

That's what Jesus did in Mark 1:33–34: "The whole town gathered at the door, and Jesus healed many who had various diseases." Very early the next morning, while it was still dark, Jesus got up, left the house, and went off to a solitary place, where he tried to get his schedule better organized.

That's not the way the passage reads, is it? That's what

I would have done. But what Jesus did was to pray.

When Peter and his companions finally located Jesus they said, "Everyone is looking for you!" (v. 37). In other words: "Oh, you've been praying. How nice! Now let's get back to the crowd waiting for you. You won't believe how big it is!"

Somewhere along the line, the apostles started to imitate their Lord. Acts 6 tells us, "In those days when the number of disciples was increasing," what the Twelve did was to give over some of their responsibilities, their busyness, in order to "give [their] attention to prayer and the ministry of the word." Apparently the example of their Lord had had an impact on their thinking.

When we, like Jesus, empower our activities with prayer, God often sees to it that impossible dreams come true. And what great joy we experience just as the fictional Amanda felt when the King came to her aid.

> He smiled at Amanda, the old, wonderful smile filled with kingslove, and for a moment it was as though they were in the Inner Circle surrounded by the dancing, leaping Sacred Flame. . . .
>
> Relief flooded Amanda. She bowed her knee in a courtly curtsey and murmured, "My Liege Lord."
>
> Then, sheltering the frightened girl in his arms, he said, "I think you had better come and be a princess in the company of my people."
>
> In short order, they piled into a waiting taxi. To Amanda's surprise, Hero was sitting in the front seat. He reached over, gave her hand a squeeze and said, "Good work." How wonderful to be fellow to a

brigade that could arrange last-minute rescues!

Amanda glanced through the open doors of the empty courtyard as the taxi pulled away. She felt relief, but—but jauntiness, too. Some of the old spirit of field and stream and childhood returned. A girl had been rescued from a terrible fate and was now nestled in the embrace of the King. No one—not Hero, not the cabbie, nor His Majesty—had scolded her with a "What-in-the-name-of-Great-Park-possessed-you?"

She smiled back at Hero and was proud because *she* did not remind him that street wise, alley smart, he had said she could do nothing. It was true. She *had* done nothing. The Names and the King had done it all—but for a field child unused to city ways, she had done nothing very well indeed!

FOR DISCUSSION AND REFLECTION

1. What Hannah-like prayer requests have people shared with you that fit the impossible dream category?

2. Do you personally hold on to any Hannah-like impossible dreams? If so, what are they?

3. How can you pray for these kinds of special requests in a way that it is to God's advantage to grant them?

4. What barriers keep you from praying the way you would like?

5. Generally speaking, is your church stronger or weaker in the discipline of prayer than you are? Explain your answer.

6. What would you like to learn about prayer from someone stronger than you? What could you teach about prayer to someone less experienced than you are?

READINGS

If we are involved in the marketplace, we are trained to believe that time is money. That's why we talk about managing time, using it efficiently and profitably, and—as a result of our concern—dealing with time pressures.

Cram more in. Start earlier. Work later. Take work home. Dictate on the commuter train. Make phone calls in the car. Use a laptop computer in airports. Schedule breakfasts, lunches and dinners for profit. Performance, performance, performance—it's the key to promotion, to compensation increase, to power.

If an ordinary car engine turns four thousand revolutions per minute, a racing motor can turn up to ten thousand. The marketplace mentality says, "Rev that engine up to ten thousand as soon as you get up in the morning, and keep it there until you collapse in the sack at night."

Getting caught in that intense pace can be rewarding! It's exciting when the adrenaline starts to flow and you get on a roll, when your motor starts racing faster and faster. But it leaves precious little time for quiet moments with God.

You don't have to be in business to be overcommitted. Women with small children know what it means to do ten thousand RPMs all day long. Almost every minute of every day is consumed by those little creatures who pull on your pants legs, color on your walls, track mud on your carpet, throw food on your floor and then have the audacity to fuss in the middle of the night.

The pace of single, working parents is double or triple that of the rest of us. It is incomprehensible to me how they can meet the incessant demands of work all day and then go home to face the even more incessant demands of their children, with never any time out.

I see pastors, elders, church board members operating at the same relentless pace as everyone else. Never a dull moment; never a reflective moment either. Frightened, I ask myself, *Where does the still, small voice of God fit into our hectic lives? When do we allow Him to lead and guide and correct and affirm? And if this seldom or never happens, how can we lead truly authentic Christian lives?*

Too Busy Not to Pray,
Bill Hybels, InterVarsity, pages 98–99.

•••

In an era of anxiety and opportunities in which time is one of the most carefully guarded personal resources, why would people commit time to pray to a God with whom relatively few of them have a personal, life-defining relationship? Quite simply, Americans believe that prayer works. Americans are practical in using their resources. Those endeavors that demonstrate or maintain the promise of a good return on the investment of resources will continue to reap a commitment of those resources. Prayer, to date, meets the standard.

Almost 6 out of 10 adults (56%) say they are "absolutely certain" that prayer rally makes a difference in their lives. An additional 1 out of 4 adults (23%) are "somewhat certain." Overall, this is 8 out of 10 people who remain at least partially persuaded that prayer has the power to affect their lives in a real way.

Interestingly, one out of five people who pray perceive prayer to be a gamble. They contend that they have no assurance or confidence in the power of prayer to make a difference, but they are hopeful it will work on their behalf.

"Look, it's a tough world out there. Does prayer really work? How would I know? How would anybody know? It's a chance you take, but I figure it doesn't cost me anything and it can't hurt. It's kinda like playin' the lottery. You lose, you haven't lost much. You win, you hit the jackpot, and it's all worth it."

There may be reason to doubt whether many who pray are doing so with total confidence, but a surprisingly low proportion (just 11%) say they generally rely upon prayer as a last resort in difficult times. Rather, four out of five praying adults (82%) said that prayer is a regular part of their lives, regardless of the circumstances in which they find themselves.

Among the adults who pray to God, the frequency of their prayers is surprising. Almost 6 out of 10 (58%) claim that they pray every day. Just 1% state that they pray less than once a week; the rest of the respondents were distributed fairly evenly in terms of how many days a week they pray. Again, the types of people most likely to pray daily included women, nonwhites, churched people and Christians. Add to that senior citizens, people of lesser means and Protestants, and you have the segments most committed to regular prayer sessions. The types of people who stand out as the least likely to pray during the course of a week are residents of the Northeast and suburbanites.

When people pray, they usually pray more than once during the day. Among the people who pray, half (52%) say they usually pray more than once during the days they speak with God; 8% say that it varies, sometimes more than once, sometimes once; and about 4 out of 10 claim they typically pray once during those days they pray at all.

For most people, prayer is not a prolonged activity. The average amount of time adults spend in prayer is about 5 minutes. Overall, the study discovered that 1 out of 14 people (7%) who pray claim their average prayer time lasts between 15 and 30 minutes; another 6% stated that they usually prayed for more than 30 minutes each time they pray.

Absolute Confusion,
George Barna, Regal, pages 95–96.

CHAPTER FIVE
CONFRONT YOUR
UNGODLY PREJUDICES

Maybe you're like I am. Every so often you have a dream that really troubles you. For example, here's a recurring nightmare of mine I recall from years back. I would be watching from the last row of an auditorium as a magician performed illusions. He would ask for a volunteer to come up, and one of my young sons, who was sitting down in front, would respond. He would be put in a box through which a sword was to be thrust. But suddenly I knew the trick wasn't going to work, and my son would actually be killed. So I'd race to the front, trying to stop things, but I would always be too late. I'd hear a piercing scream, at which point I'd wake up, terrified.

Usually I don't recall my dreams. But I had this one more than once, and it was troubling enough to remember.

I'm told that one's dreams are usually not about somebody else, like my young son, but about oneself. With that perspective, I eventually became aware that this dream was underscoring what God had been telling me though a number of different means. There were little-boy aspects of my personality that needed to be put to death. If I didn't stop acting like a little boy in some ways, the Lord would never be able to trust me with certain adult assignments. I feel I've heeded those warnings from the Lord and done the work he wanted to accomplish. And, interestingly, that dream hasn't returned.

Confronted by the Lord

In Scripture, we see that Peter had one of those unusual revelations from the Lord while he was in Joppa.

> About noon the following day as they were on their journey and approaching the city, Peter went up on the roof to pray. He became hungry and wanted something to eat, and while the meal was being prepared, he fell into a trance. He saw heaven opened and something like a large sheet being let down to earth by its four corners. It contained all kinds of four-footed animals, as well as reptiles of the earth and birds of the air. Then a voice told him, "Get up, Peter. Kill and eat."
>
> "Surely not, Lord!" Peter replied. "I have never eaten anything impure or unclean."
>
> The voice spoke to him a second time, "Do not call anything impure that God has made clean."
>
> This happened three times, and immediately the sheet was taken back to heaven. . . .
>
> While Peter was still thinking about the vision, the Spirit said to him, "Simon, three men are looking for you. So get up and go downstairs. Do not hesitate to go with them, for I have sent them."

> Peter went down and said to the men, "I'm the
> one you're looking for. Why have you come?" (Acts
> 10:9–16, 19–21).

It was then he learned they had been sent by a Gentile named Cornelius, a centurion in what was called the Italian regiment. "He is a righteous and God-fearing men, who is respected by all the Jewish people," they said. "A holy angel told him to have you come to his house so that he could hear what you have to say" (v. 22).

The Lord was preparing Peter to be responsive to the invitation of this Gentile he normally wouldn't even have associated with. That's because God wanted his apostles to extend the message of his kingdom beyond the Jewish world. To do that, to get these servants of his to buy into his more expansive dream, the Lord had to somehow break through certain prejudices they held.

Peter figured out the puzzle of his vision a lot faster than I did the message of my dream. He had to, because before long he found himself at the home of Cornelius, preaching Christ and seeing the Holy Spirit fall upon the group. The Scriptures report:

> While Peter was still speaking these words, the
> Holy Spirit came on all who heard the message. The
> circumcised believers [or, the Jewish believers] who
> had come with Peter were astonished that the gift of
> the Holy Spirit had been poured out even on the
> Gentiles. For they heard them speaking in tongues
> and praising God (Acts 10:44–46).

I believe it's fair to say that God forces us to confront the scandal of our prejudices when they stand in the way of the fulfillment of his dreams. The early church, which was almost exclusively Jewish, would undoubtedly have stayed that way if the Lord had not pushed his key leaders, such as Peter, and said, "Don't call anything impure that God has made clean."

Since the first century, this kind of nudging has continued through the generations. I hold the conviction that this is one of the things the Lord is trying to do in his church even today.

DOUBLE BIND

I've illustrated previous chapters with sections from *Tales of the Resistance*. The tale called "Doubletalk, Triple Tongue, and Theysay" has something to teach us about prejudice.

> Heralds stood on broadcast columns throughout Enchanted City and shouted news. They announced special events as well as the hour of the night. Because of power-outs, however, no one really knew the correct time. One herald might proclaim, "Midnight. All's well!" while another shouted "Ten–thirty o'clock. Half-night approaches!" No wonder citizens suffered from indigestion, they were always eating dinner at the wrong hour.
>
> Doubletalk, Triple Tongue, and Theysay were friends. The three boys had grown up in Moire

Oxan, the tenement slums which stretched for miles, hovel stacked upon hovel. Together they endured illness, poverty, hunger, and branding. When Theysay's parents died, the other two helped him escape orphan dragnets by hiding him back and forth in their own tenement hovels, at great risk of penalty to themselves.

All were now heralds of the Enchanter—and proud of their accomplishment. It was something for penniless young men to rise to heraldship, to stand on the tall broadcast columns, trusted with all the news fit to proclaim. It was something for ragtag ruffians to wear the red and yellow jerseys with the Enchanter's insignia of blazing fire. It was something to blow the herald horn whenever the wizard's sleek black limousine moved ominously through the city streets, and to shout, "The Enchanter is coming! Make way for the Enchanter!"

Unfortunately, heralds frequently made contradictory announcements. One might shout, "Melons in the marketplace! First come, first served!" while the herald on the very next post was shouting, "No melons today! Try rutabagas in your fruit salad!"

Some people suspected that heralds were chosen only if they had something wrong with their speech. Some heralds spoke backwards, "!gnimoc si retnahcnE ehT" Some had twisted tongues. Some had lockmouth, so that all s's whistled through clenched teeth with a wicked his-s-s-s-s-s. Some had very bad breath.

Doubletalk made positive announcements out of one side of his mouth. "The Enchanter is coming," for instance, or, "Melons in the marketplace!" would be announced out of the right side. Negative announcements, however, would be shouted out of the left side of his mouth: "The Enchanter is not coming!" "The melons have all been stolen!"

Trouble began when Doubletalk couldn't decide if the announcement was negative or positive. Was the theft of rutabagas good or bad news? Or, maybe, it was a good thing that the Enchanter *wasn't* coming.

Consequently, he began to make announcements out of both sides of his mouth. "The Enchanter is coming!" (on the right side) "The Enchanter is not coming!" (on the left). Then both at the same time. His tongue worked so hard it eventually split in two.

Doubletalk always worked up a sweat, but no one appreciated his great effort. People standing beneath his column shouted, "Heh, bub! Make up yer mind. Whatcha got? Wet-noodle brains?" And they threw rotten tomatoes.

Double talk—one thing out of one side of the mouth and something else out of the other side. Contradictory announcements.

—Witness to your non-Christian friends, but don't associate with too many non-Christians or you might compromise your convictions.

—Treat all people with Christian love—except African-Americans who move into your neighborhood, because then your property value might drop.

—Make use of all the gifts the Holy Spirit has

104

given you—unless, of course, you are a woman
who would violate all that is sacred if you
thought you had gifts intended only for men.

Prejudices. We still have them, don't we? I see them
often standing in the way of the dreams God has for the
world.

PERSONAL CRAM COURSE

Have you ever tried to master some difficult subject by
taking a cram course? Perhaps in a short period of time
you were going to learn how to speak French or become
an accomplished pianist.

What happened?

I could say I took a 12-year inner city cram course on
racial reconciliation. Now, for some, 12 years might seem
too long for a cram course. But when we realize that
racism in this land has been hundreds of years in the
making, 12 years is actually rather a short period of time
in which to expect to master the subject!

What happened was that I founded an inner-city,
interracial church that quickly grew to a Sunday morning attendance of 500. On my staff were a Chinese
Filipino man, an African-American man, and also a
Caucasian woman. We did well, for a while—about eight
years. But eventually all the blacks left. I confess that I,
as senior minister, was as much involved and to blame
for what happened as anyone. In retrospect, I would say

I flunked the racial reconciliation course. On the other hand, I certainly learned a great deal, probably as much about my flaws as anything! So when I talk about personal racism or racism in the church, it's not just another topic to me.

That church ministry began in 1967. At that time in Chicago, there was minimal communication between the black church and the white church. Today, in this third largest of U.S. cities, there are ministries where blacks and whites work together in the church beautifully. I applaud those efforts. In fact, I stand and applaud. I rejoice. I shout, "Praise the Lord!"

But the truth is, when you look at the broader church picture, not much progress has been made toward racial reconciliation. When it comes to blacks and whites working together, the church lags behind the sports world, the entertainment world, the world of education, the world of business, the world of government, and on and on.

There's a strong white church, there's a strong black church, and there's a strong Latino church. But there isn't nearly as much of a coming together racially as we might like to think. Most honest church leaders would say that as Christians we're probably 15 to 20 years behind where we should be on this issue.

Don't misunderstand me. I'm not equating the church with the Ku Klux Klan. I'm not overlooking the fact that some progress has been made. I'm just honestly pointing out that Christians should be a lot further along than we are in terms of racial reconciliation.

Most churches or parachurch organizations are not in a position to boast. More likely, they admit to finding the race issue an extremely difficult problem to work through. But if Christians ever expect to be heard as a viable voice in Chicago or in this nation or in North America, then racism in the church must be addressed. It's a glass ceiling that needs to be shattered, and soon.

My conviction is that God still forces his people to confront their prejudices when they stand in the way of his dreams becoming reality. As we plead with the Spirit for revival *in the church*, I believe this is one of the sins he will convict us of. Daring to dream again means breaking through the racial barriers that hold us back.

GETTING TOGETHER

Another prejudice that needs to be addressed is our denominationalism. I'm not necessarily advocating that we join together as part of a great ecumenical movement. We don't need to blindly embrace the minister down the street who believes Christ was a good man but little more—and certainly not the unique Son of God. There are essential doctrinal differences that cannot be overlooked.

But that doesn't mean that all in the true body of Christ, those who have received his saving grace, can't learn to work together better. In our land the enemy is increasing in power. The strides Satan has made in recent

107

years are frightening. Christians will never stop him if we can't learn to cooperate more.

I am thrilled with reports I hear of ministers in many parts of the country praying together across denominational lines. We are not as far behind denominationally as we are racially, but that's hardly a high compliment.

As I talk with church leaders, I am amazed how little Baptists know about Episcopalians, or Episcopalians about the Salvation Army, or the Army about what's happening in Presbyterian circles. In many ways these are like different worlds that seldom interface unless something like a Billy Graham Crusade brings them together.

In a given town, churches and the people of those various churches so often are spiritually isolated from one another. Free Methodists don't know who attends the local Church of God or the Missouri Synod Lutheran church or the Evangelical Free church or the Assembly of God church. There are exceptions, but on the whole we don't really know the body of Christ in our particular settings as I believe the Lord would like us to.

Are times changing? I hope so. It's never too late to dream. But, I wonder, will minor differences or our fears of one another continue to keep us apart so that we'll never know how strong we could have been, if only we had worked harder at being unified?

Let's face the facts. It still befuddles the average non-Christian that the church has so many divisions. If Christians agree on the greater portion of their beliefs, why don't they concentrate on that, rather than on their differences? Let's wake up. Our divisions absolutely bamboozle nonbelievers! We Christians should be equally concerned.

I have preached in many different denominational settings. I've never yet found a group I didn't like—never! Mennonites, Wesleyans, Nazarenes, Friends, Moravians: They're all wonderful people. Lord, bring us together.

I believe he wants to do just that. I truly am convinced God is almost forcing us to confront this scandal of our denominational prejudices, because it stands in the way of his dreams for us.

There are so many Scriptures that speak to issues like these. In 1 Corinthians 1, Paul writes: "One of you says, 'I follow Paul' another, 'I follow Apollos'; another, 'I follow Cephas'; still another, 'I follow Christ.' Is Christ divided?" the apostle asks in wonderment (vv. 12–13).

SHARING THE BURDEN

A passage like John 4 reveals the racism of New Testament times as we see the Samaritan woman responding to Christ, "How can you ask me for a drink?" John, the author, adds parenthetically, "(for Jews do not associate with Samaritans)." But Jesus did anyway (v. 9).

Also revealing is verse 27 of that chapter. When the disciples returned to the scene, the Scriptures record, they were surprised, not that Jesus was talking to a Samaritan, but that our Lord was conversing with a woman!

I believe we still have lessons to learn from Christ on this matter. In Luke 8, referring to Jesus' travels from one town and village to another, we read, "The Twelve were with him, and also some women" (vv. 1–2). The passage names three of them: Mary Magdalene, Susanna, and Joanna. Joanna's husband, Cuza, was the manager of Herod's household. So the wife of the king's steward was traveling with Jesus as he preached!

According to Luke 8:3, "These women were helping to support them [the disciples] out of their own means." Ministry requires money, and apparently a lot of it was being provided by the women who traveled with Christ.

Contrary to the practices of the day, Jesus opened up places of service like this for women. It was risky. There could have been a lot of misunderstandings about women traveling with his ministry team. But Jesus didn't exclude them. I believe we too need to open up more places for women to use their special resources for kingdom work.

With that statement I haven't tried to resolve all the issues related to women in ministry. But I am challenging men of the church to make more room at the table for women, just as we need to do for other ethnic groups. Can you respond "amen" to that?

For too long we have stereotyped women as being capable of taking charge of the church nursery but not the church treasury. We've said women can teach boys and girls but not a mixed adult class. In Scripture we read that women should learn in silence. Often the only word we see is "silence." We miss the fact that women were encouraged to inquire and learn. Why learn if one's knowledge can't be used?

One of the great unsung demonstrations of the Holy Spirit's work in the North American church is what's happening among women. They are becoming "maiden warriors." I commend my sisters in the Lord. And I believe the Lord is challenging many of us who are men to confront our sexual prejudices.

This chapter has been a cram course. I've tried to write too much in too restricted a space. Suffice it to underscore that this matter of prejudices is a real-life nightmare that continues to trouble the church. The Lord is telling me to grow up and stop acting out of little-boy fears. What's he saying to you?

FOR DISCUSSION AND REFLECTION

1. Are there prejudices in the North American church that still grieve the heart of God? If so, what are they?

2. Sincere Christians sometimes reinforce their prejudices by appealing to Scripture. How is this possible?

3. In an effort to overcome prejudice and show love and understanding, Christians can sometimes

111

compromise what Scripture teaches. Give an example of how this might happen.

4. Who are people or groups you have prejudged or were prejudiced toward in the past?

5. Has the Holy Spirit been revealing any new prejudices you need to correct? What has God been showing you?

6. When it comes to tearing down walls of prejudice, do you see the church in North America as ahead of or behind the secular culture? Why? Give examples if you can.

READINGS

Director Spike Lee's movie Malcolm X hit the theaters in 1992, spawning a revival of the Black Muslim leader's controversial and powerful rhetoric of the sixties (not to mention X hats and tee shirts sprouting from coast to coast). In one scene in the movie, a white coed approaches Malcolm X as he arrives on the campus of Harvard University to give a speech. She assures him that even though she's white, she's sympathetic to his cause.

"What can someone like me do to help?" she asks earnestly.

"Nothing," he answers coldly.

Part of Malcolm X's great appeal to the black community was that he stood up for black self-determination. He challenged blacks to stay in school, get off drugs, get off welfare, get a job, and take responsibility for their families. But unlike Martin Luther King, Jr., who walked hand in hand with whites as he challenged the American conscience, Malcolm's message—at that time—was: "We don't need whites to make it." Many blacks still believe that. They desire independence and disdain whites as controllers.

In the realm of Christian fellowship and effective growth in the church, many still believe blacks and whites can go their independent ways and remain effective. In the mid-'80s, C. Peter Wagner of the Church

Growth Institute at Fuller Theological Seminary in Pasadena, California, published two books discussing the factors that characterize growing churches. One of the more controversial principles growing out of the Institute's research is the homogeneous factor—that is, people feel most comfortable with people like themselves; therefore, churches must take this human tendency into account if they wish to draw in new members.

Wagner is partially correct; the human tendency is to seek those like ourselves. "Birds of a feather do flock together," and when it comes to church, Christians generally sort themselves out by race, class, and culture. It's not only black and white, either. Most Georgia farmers would feel quite out of place in a highbrow Episcopal service; Cambodian refugees are forming their own congregations under the umbrella of a sponsoring American church; Spanish-speaking and Korean congregations feel the need to preserve their distinctiveness.

Do we need each other? Those who believe in "homogeneous churches" and "niche marketing" or Afro-centrism and self-determination don't necessarily think so. Other than trying to avoid race riots, why should we go through all the grief necessary to achieve racial reconciliation? Why fight human nature? Why not just let "them" have their church, and "we" will have our church?

The real question, however, is do we solidify the human tendency to flock together with our own kind into a "principle" for the body of Christ? Do we accept a "separate but equal" mind-set for Christian fellowship and relationship?

114

Our answer is no. We cannot get along without each other if the body of Christ is to be salt and light to a world torn apart by racial strife. The principle of interdependence recognizes our differences but realizes that we each bring something to the table that the other person needs, resulting in equality (key verses: 2 Corinthians 8:12–14). Interdependence demonstrates the transforming nature of the gospel and declares that we do need each other if we are to live out the ministry of reconciliation. (Where would the gospel be today if Christ's disciples throughout the centuries had not accepted his challenge to be ambassadors of reconciliation across racial and cultural barriers?)

Breaking Down Walls,
Raleigh Washington and Glen Kehrein, Moody, pages 169–71.

•••

I am a graduate of four distinctly conservative institutions—Bob Jones University, Reformed Episcopal Seminary, Covenant Theological Seminary, and Concordial Theological Seminary. I am also a professor of theology at Wheaton College and Graduate School, an evangelical institution known for its conservative point of view.

As you might expect, I have been decidedly influenced by my experiences at these various institutions and the church groups they represent. And, as the philosopher

115

Hans-Georg Gadamer would say, I carry around with me these influences as well as influences from home and from life in general. Gadamer calls these experiences "prejudices." I have, you might say, a conditioning within me that I cannot completely overcome; I hold prejudices from such diverse sources as fundamentalism, Calvinism, Lutheranism, and evangelicalism. These points of view influence the way I think about the Christian faith and the way I worship.

All of us—and our churches—have dispositions of this sort. It's not that we are intentionally prejudiced. Instead, the environments in which we were raised and in which we have worshiped build within us convictions that we may not even be able to identify.

For example, the nonliturgical background of my early years naturally made me skeptical about both the liturgical and charismatic traditions of worship. I was suspicious of anyone who did not believe or practice the Christian faith as I did. And I was dead certain that I was right and they were wrong.

These prejudices became ingrained during my years at home and my formative years in college. I can point to an incident when I was twelve years old that surely built prejudice within me. The story goes like this: A Reformed couple came to our Baptist parsonage to visit with my parents. As they were deeply engaged in conversation about some religious matter—the favorite topic in my home—the male visitor lighted a cigarette right there in our living room. I was shocked. How could someone talk about religion and smoke at the same time?

As soon as our guests left, I quickly made my way to my mother's side. "Mother, I thought those people were Christians. How can somebody smoke and be a Christian?" My mother's answer was classic: "Well, Robert, they are Reformed. And Reformed people, though they are Christian, have funny ideas and do worldly things. But we are Baptists, the best of the Christian groups. We don't have funny ideas and aren't worldly." Right then and there, in that young and impressionable mind, a prejudice was set in place.

I had similar experiences in college. I can, for example, distinctly remember the founder of the college cupping his hands over his mouth in chapel and crying, "Do you want to know where a man stands with God?" Obviously anyone who is spiritual sensitive wants to know how to determine a person's standing with God. I leaned forward, anxiously awaiting his answer. "You only have to ask that person one question," he continued. Then, after a moment's pause, came the confident, dogmatic assertion, "Ask him, 'What do you think of this university?'"

Now I was aware of how people felt about that university. Some thought the school was reactionary, racist, legalistic, dogmatic, and arrogant. "What about those people?" I thought. "Is God angry with them? Have they really fallen away from the truth?" As I recalled other assertions I'd heard proclaimed at the college, I found myself asking, "Is everybody in the World Council of Churches an apostate renegade seeking to destroy the

117

true church? Are all liturgical people really ritualists, servants of a dead orthodoxy given to vain repetition? Is the charismatic movement really of the devil?" With all of these questions, I was dealing with prejudices that had long ago been planted in my mind like seeds placed in the rich, dark soil of a spring garden.

Signs of Wonder,
Robert Webber, Abbot Martyn, pages 6–7.

•••

The needs, potential, and qualifications of women have been shrouded in the mists of interminable squabbles about women's roles in the church. Whatever your view about these matters, our fights have done nothing to erase the deeply ingrained prejudices of men toward women. We cannot continue our rather brutish behavior, thinking that our patient Christian wives, friends, and fellow workers don't really care. We mistakenly assume that because they are not radical feminists they have no feelings.

Change begins with our language, because what we say and what we write reveals our unchallenged assumptions about women. Beyond that, however, we must change our missions commitment to include evangelizing and training the world's women. Women leaders from Africa and Asia have correctly exposed the blind side of church and mission strategies in this regard. If we contemplate new ministries, without taking into account the huge potential for significant leadership among Christian women, we enter the field with one arm cut off.

Too often we act as if missions history means nothing. How many times do we ring the changes on William Carey, Hudson Taylor, and Jim Elliot, without ever mentioning Mary Slessor, Gladys Aylward, and Helen Roseveare. What does such oversight say to women in our schools and churches? If mission work sounds like the private domain of an exclusive men's club, we aren't going to attract capable women.

Perhaps the strongest signal we send women is the role we give, or do not give, to them in mission leadership. Some of our institutions would be better served if the wives of the men in charge were given the job. In these cases, the wife is gifted in management and administration, while her husband's gifts are in teaching, preaching, and counseling. The point is to use people in their strengths, regardless of their sex. The work of God could be considerably expedited if we got serious about developing women for leadership in world missions.

Men, it's long past the time to change.

"Men: It's Time to Change," James Reapsome
Pulse, 9 October 1991. Used by permission.

CHAPTER SIX
IDENTIFY WITH GOD'S HEART FOR THE WORLD

People don't like it when somebody does them dirty. Most write their enemies off. They usually aren't open to extending any form of friendship to them. Given the opportunity to return the ill favor, they relish doing what they can to make life harder for those who have hurt them. The thought that someday maybe they could be good friends is the last thing they would dream of.

But that's not how the Lord is! His dreams for all who have offended him is that someday they would be wooed back into a loving relationship. God's dreams are incredible in that regard.

Jonah was a prophet who found out the hard way what God's heart is like. The last thing in the world he wanted to do was to hold a preaching crusade in Nineveh, capital of Assyria. Talk about a rotten assignment!

Think about it: Would you as a North American want to preach Christ in an open-air crusade next week in Baghdad? How do you suppose Saddam Hussein would feel about it? That's the kind of challenge God gave Jonah. Assyria was the most feared nation of his day— the reigning superpower. And, unlike modern-day Iraq,

NEVER TOO LATE TO DREAM

Assyria hadn't been defeated in a relatively recent war.

In the second verse of the small Old Testament book that bears this prophet's name, God says, "Go to the great city of Nineveh and preach against it, because its wickedness has come up before me."

It most certainly was a great capital city. Its size was huge for that time: 600,000 inhabitants, all living comfortably behind 100-foot-high protective walls—and serving their own gods.

Destined to later destroy the ten northern tribes of Israel on the way to becoming an awesome world empire, these people had a reputation that was frightening. No other conquerors treated their vanquished so cruelly. They were barbaric and inhumane.

"Lord, if I do what you're requesting," Jonah might well have responded, "I'll be in a no-win situation. In the first place, it's unlikely they'll listen to any Jewish preacher. And though I don't mind jeers or a few rotten eggs, torture doesn't really appeal to me!"

You see, the Assyrians were known for ramming a sharp stake up through the chest of a prisoner, quickly planting the stake in a hole in the ground, and then laughing while the victim squirmed until dead. That was the means of execution if the prisoner was lucky. History teaches that more often than not, captives would be tied spread-eagle on the ground and slowly skinned alive!

A GOD TOO MERCIFUL

I can picture Jonah reminding God, "Come on, now, I have no stomach for that kind of stuff! What's that? . . .

You're sure they'll listen to what I say? I can't imagine it, God. But let's just say they do, and they momentarily repent. I lose again. Because I know exactly what's going to happen. I can see it coming. Even a little godly sorrow on their part, some sniffles and a few tears, and you won't destroy them. That's it. I'm right, I know I am. I know you very well, God. You're too merciful. Your heart's too big. Do you think those people will respect you if you don't send a white blast of fire against at least a major portion of their city? Listen to me. Why be kind to them, God? They don't love you. Forget about these foreigners; they're not worth it. All they've ever given you or your people is dirt."

So that you won't think I'm making up Jonah's thoughts, let me quote from the last chapter of this short book. Jonah had already had his whale experience. That's what finally made him willing to take on God's assignment. So he preached, and—lo and behold—the Ninevites repented in sackcloth and ashes. And, sure enough, in chapter 3, verse 10, we read: "When God saw what they did and how they turned from their evil ways, he had compassion and did not bring upon them the destruction he had threatened."

Jonah was steaming.

> But Jonah was greatly displeased and became angry. He prayed to the Lord, "O Lord, is this not what I said when I was still at home? That is why I was so quick to flee to Tarshish. I knew that you are a gracious and compassionate God, slow to anger

> and abounding in love, a God who relents from
> sending calamity" (Jonah 4:1–3).

In other words, Jonah was telling God, "You don't
treat people dirty even when that's how they act toward
you. And that really frosts me!"

This account ends with God's pointing out to this
prophet that "Nineveh has more than a hundred and
twenty thousand people who cannot tell their right hand
from their left. Should I not be concerned about that
great city?" What most commentators believe this means
is that there were 120,000 children in this place. So calm
down, Jonah. You might just overlook that fact when
you ask for judgment fire to fall, but God can't. "And,
yes, I love these people," the Lord was saying to Jonah.
"I just wish you cared about them too."

I fear that the North American church today is quite
often like Jonah. We care about our own countries but
not for much beyond our borders. Our spiritual dreams
might include the growth of our local church and the
denomination to which it belongs, but only a small percentage of Christians identify with God's great heart of
love for other nations. This is especially true when we
think about nations considered to be our enemies.

We may even be a bit turned off when we hear chal-
lenges based on Christ's last words. Just prior to his
ascension, Jesus said, "Go and make disciples of all
nations . . . teaching them to obey everything I have
commanded you" (Matt. 28:19–20). Apparently he

wanted us to begin to think globally.

Here's how that commission comes out in Acts. "But you will receive power when the Holy Spirit comes on you; and you will be my witnesses in Jerusalem, and in all Judea and Samaria, and to the ends of the earth" (1:8). This includes places with foreign (even Assyrian-sounding) names like Mozambique, Afghanistan, Yemen, Chad, Chile, Indonesia, Somalia, Ukraine, Romania, Paraguay, Nepal, Mongolia, and many more with people whose ways seem strange to us, but not to God. He loves them dearly. I didn't name one country he doesn't have intensely strong feelings for. I couldn't have named one if I'd tried.

Would you believe that it's nations other than our own where the kingdom is presently making its greatest advances? I believe it's in places foreign to us where the most exciting stories of faith are being lived out. If we remain provincial in our thinking, we are the losers. The sooner we start looking at the rest of the world, the more likely it is we will see faith being lived out in New Testament ways. So it's to our advantage to overcome the barrier of perceiving that we have all the answers, spiritually speaking.

CONCERN FOR THE INNOCENTS

We must also remember God's words to Jonah about the children, the innocents. Wherever we travel we see children. We can't just write them off. As I talk, I'm picturing the many, many children of India I've seen.

NEVER TOO LATE TO DREAM

My wife, Karen, and I sought to help readers identify with the plight of the world's children when we wrote *Tales of the Resistance*. This is from the chapter called "The Orphan Exodus," introduced in chapter 3 of this book.

> The orphan pavilion was to one side of the Dagoda, enclosed by a high wall with a surrounding courtyard. A sign beside the tall gate proclaimed "WE LOVE CHILDREN—Orphan Keepers' Association," but everyone in Enchanted City knew that children were loved only because they provided forced labor to do the dirty work of the Enchanter.
>
> Two huge wolves the size of lions guarded either side of the entrance. They growled as the men approached; they bared their teeth and drooled. A soft light gathered around the King. The wolves stared, whimpered, and the hid their heads in their paws while the two men passed them by. All closed places opened to the King when he so willed it.
>
> Inside, a squad of orphans wearing tattered rags scrubbed the courtyard. A keeper's assistant with a whistle around her neck chanted, "Clean-clean-clean!" and stood ready to beat the slow workers with a long stick. Another work detail, a long line of children tied together at the ankles with rough sections of rope, were getting ready to collect the city garbage which citizens tossed on the street. A whistle blew— *Hweet! Hweet!*—and the crew marched to the waiting carts while another assistant prodded them with the sharp tines of her forked shovel.
>
> Huge vats of water boiled while children stirred the dirty clothes within. The hot water splashed on

the orphans' rags, burning them one moment and
then soaking them to the skin in the cold night. An
assistant prodded them with a long wooden turning
spoon. *Hweet!* She blew her whistle and shouted,
"Scoundrels! Dimwits! I'll boil *you* if you spill any
more wash water!" *Hweet!*

All the orphans, boys and girls, wore the same
haircuts, making it nearly impossible to tell one from
another. Their clothes were an identical gray which
grew increasingly threadbare during washings as they
were passed down from one child to another. Skinny,
sad eyed, covered with sores from the lack of proper
foods, not one orphan smiled or laughed or told
jokes or chased another in games of tag. Games were
forbidden, and play had been outlawed. No one
belonged to any other—brothers and sisters were
separated. There were no holidays and never any
birthday cakes.

Children are hardly the people to blame for the problems of the world. Even so, many children, through no
fault of their own, live very sad lives. For example, studies show that every year more than a million children
worldwide are coerced into prostitution, pornography, or
other forms of sexual exploitation. The number of home-
less children in the world is also in the millions.

People don't generally know that in our lifetime children in many settings have been forced to fight in adult
wars. Between fifty and one hundred thousand children
died in combat in the Iran/Iraq war. Sometimes these
youngsters were used to clear mines. They were tied
together and obliged to walk across Iraqi mine fields to

detonate explosives so that the regular army could proceed unharmed.

Closer to home, reports of children being forced to fight adult wars have come out of Central American countries such as Nicaragua, Guatemala, and El Salvador.

CALLING CHILDREN IN LOVE

The Lord has a most tender heart for children. "Red and yellow, black and white, they are precious in his sight. Jesus loves the little children of the world." But many of the world's children will never hear about this love unless someone goes and tells them about our Lord. They will not grow up as my four children did, having heard about the Savior from a very early age.

I now have six grandchildren. The youngest, Ayden, is only two years old. He's being raised in a loving Christian home and already regularly attends church. But millions upon millions of innocent children and grandchildren—little sons and daughters, beautiful grandsons and granddaughters—all with names and feelings and smiles and great potential for good and bad, will never hear about Christ unless someone goes to tell them the news that God dearly loves them.

I'd like to return to the story, "The Orphan Exodus."

> "I am the Orphan Keeper," she intoned. "You will do my bidding. You will keep my commands. I have control over your lives and your destinies. I am the one who says yea and nay. You can never escape. You can never go where I say no."

The children cowered, even the older ones. All knew this loveless woman had power to send them to the underworld, to poison their food and call it nightailment, to advance them or to cut off their rations. It was she who ordered punishment for all if one orphan misbehaved.

"You are mine! You are all mine!" she shouted again, lashing the air with the hand whip.

"LET MY CHILDREN GO!"

Everyone within the courtyard froze. The drums stopped in mid-roll *tatatata—TA?* Who dared disrupt the Orphan Keeper's time schedule? Who dared interrupt her early night-work-duty harangue? The children shivered in the cold, miserable with hunger and now with dread. What torture would they suffer because of this unspeakable challenge?

The King had shouted the words. He faced the Orphan Keeper, throwing the hood of his common garment back from his head as though she would recognize him once his face was fully revealed in the torchlight. The children gasped at such defiance. Who was this man?

The King's hair glimmered with gold highlights and his loosened street robe fell to the paving stones and he stood strong and tall and broad shouldered and handsome. Big Operator gasped—he had never beheld his King undisguised, so young and so beautiful.

The Orphan Keeper cracked her cat-o'-nine-tails in the air. "I know you, you troublemaker. You instigator! Who do you think you are, challenging my power? The Enchanter has cast his spell over these children. They are mine! I can do what I please with them."

129

The King answered her not a word, but all could see he was as angry as she. He crossed the pavement and lifted his hands. A wind began to blow, around and around, *who-hooooo-ooo; who-hooooo-ooo.* It caught the torches of the torchbearers and bound the flames in one windy firebrand—*who-hooooo-ooo; who-hooooo-ooo!* Up—up!—it shot into the night sky over the orphan pavilion, blazing. By its light all could see the King grab the hand whip from the Orphan Keeper's grasp, lash the pokers from the Burners' hands, scatter the assistants with a crack, and then toss the instruments of torture to the sky. A bolt of lightning flashed from nowhere, striking with a CRA—A—A—CK! Flames burst and a ball of fire fell to the ground, finally to be extinguished at the Orphan Keeper's feet.

The ranks of orphans gasped. The assistant keepers hid their prodding spoons, sticks, and shovels behind their backs, dropped them to the ground, or pushed them under carts.

Then in the unlit dark all could see the warm radiance of the man standing in the middle of the courtyard, daring to defy the evil power of the Orphan Keeper herself. The King signaled to Big Operator and together, with a mighty thrust, they overturned the boiling vat of palace laundry. They ripped the wheels from the work carts, their muscles straining in a fury of indignation.

And no one moved to stop them. The Burners stood mesmerized. No warning signal was given to the Dagoda. The Orphan Keeper hissed as though air was escaping from her lungs—*s-s-s-s-s-s-s-s.*

Many of the children dropped to their knees, clasping their hands together beneath their chins, scarcely daring to hope. Was this one who could save them? Would their misery finally end? Was freedom close?

The King straightened himself again and stared the Orphan Keeper in the eyes. "You mistake yourself, madame," he said. His voice was tight with controlled wrath. "These children are not yours; they belong to me."

With those words he motioned to Big Operator, who stepped forward, wiping axle grease from his hands on his overalls. He bent his knee and bowed. Though comrade to the King before, he was an obedient subject now.

"Is the taxi vanguard ready?" asked the King.

"Yes, my Lord. Ready and waiting." His voice was full of satisfaction.

At that the Orphan Keeper screamed, staggering on her feet. "S-s-s-s. You!—you! You can't take thes-s-s-e children! They're waifs-s-s-s-s! They're slaves-s-s-s! The wolves-s-s-s will tear them to shreds-s-s-s-s. They do my bidding! They won't come with you! S-s-s-s."

Paying no attention, the King lifted his crossed arms and spread them in a circle about his head. More light diffused from his stretching embrace, till it filled every corner of the grim courtyard. The orphans' frozen feet began to warm; their cold, wet garments began to dry; their wounds and sores began to heal in the gentle light. Their hearts began to mend.

"What you don't understand, madame," said the King, "is that *every* orphan answers when his name is called in love."

Then the King began to call their names, names

131

unspoken for months, for years, names they themselves had almost forgotten. He called them in family
groups, brothers and sisters, brothers and brothers,
sisters and sisters, according to age and position. He
spoke their names with tenderness, with kindly affection, with cherished intimacy as though he had been
practicing them for years.

"Kristen, Ned, James, Sara, and Susan.

Anne, Ted, John, and Linda.

Jason and Maria.

Alex, Sharon, and Rob.

Eric, Jane, and Cathy.

Diane . . ."

And each child remembered his or her name. And
each child stepped from the ranks. He was more
than a number, more than flesh for the meat grinder
of the Enchanter's labor machines. He had a name
chosen in love and a family history and a King who
was worthy of service.

Can this fictional account of Christ's making children's
lives easier be lived out in reality in many places of the
world? I trust it's not too late to dream that this remains
a possibility.

GATEWAY TO THE HEART

Children have an amazing ability to capture the hearts
of adults. I recall an enchanting dirty-faced little beggar
girl I encountered some years ago near the Gateway of
India, Bombay's principal landmark and tourist attraction.

She could beg in I don't know how many languages.

She would wait long enough to catch the language she thought you were speaking. Then she would come up and make her appeal in the few words she thought you would understand. "Money please—hungry—nice man."

I would have taken her home with me if I could. I really would have. That little lady, maybe five or six years old, found a soft-hearted American in me. I gave her money, but I often wonder what her ultimate fate was.

God's final attempt to get Jonah to identify with his concern for the great city of Nineveh was an appeal based on the 120,000 innocent children living there. Scripture doesn't say what the prophet's final response was.

I also have tried to use the appeal of children as a gateway to your heart. I hope these little ones will open modern Jonahs to the multitudes of lost folk in Nineveh-like settings foreign to us. All these people, both young and old, are God's children.

His incredible dream is to reach out to them all. And God wants us to identify both with his heart and with his command to take the message of his love to all parts of the globe. As we sing in the hymn, he wants his kingdom to spread "from shore to shore." He wants to reign "wher-e'er the sun does his successive journeys run." This is what God dares to dream.

FOR DISCUSSION AND REFLECTION

1. Grade yourself on a scale of 1 to 10 (10 being best) as to how interested you are in people of countries other than your own. Explain the reason for your mark.

2. What is a country you would like to know more about? What about that country interests you?

3. From what you have read or heard, check three of the following continents where rapid church growth is being experienced:

   __ Africa
   __ Asia
   __ Australia
   __ Europe
   __ North America
   __ South America

Compare and explain your answers.

4. Give three reasons why North American Christians should become more global in their thinking.

5. What obstacles keep you from starting to become a world-class Christian?

6. How might you benefit personally from becoming more globally aware?

134

READINGS

Ramji is small of stature and of dark complexion. He lives in a one-room house made of sun-baked clay. His ancestors are the aborigines of Western India. His language is an unwritten tongue called Mouchi. Ramji ekes out starvation rations for his family from a small parcel of overworked, undernourished soil which has been passed down the family line for generations. Jungle roots and occasional chunks of wild boar meat supplement the family diet.

Waghdev, the tiger god, is Ramji's tribal deity. His sincere devotion to Waghdev is astounding. Though he has never seen a Hindu hymnal, Ramji can be heard singing the praises of his deity at almost any time of the day. Though he has never read any books about Waghdev, he has an amazing wealth of information concerning him.

Ramji has never studied for the priesthood, yet he faithfully offers sacrifices to his god. He is as meticulous about the place, the time and the way in which he carries out his religious ceremonies as if he were guided by a manual of ritual. His annual blood offering (a slain chicken) is made in the hope that the tiger god will not molest his one pair of bullocks and 11 goats.

Strange, isn't it, that you have never heard of Waghdev

when there are so many like Ramji who worship him so devoutly? No, it's not strange at all, for Waghdev is only a tribal deity. He is worshiped within the confines of a small geographic circle. Nor have his devotees ever dreamed of the necessity of proclaiming his virtues to others. Waghdev's responsibilities are definitely localized.

As a missionary to India, it has been my privilege to gather information on numerous tribal deities. Frankly, the more I have learned about most of them, the more thankful I've been that their influence is circumscribed. But I have become more and more concerned about one particular tribe of people. Numerically they are a much larger group than any Indian tribe of which I knew. They are widely scattered and possess a great diversity of languages.

The religion of the group which concerns me has little in common with the other religions of the world. There is, however, one apparent similarity between the followers of Waghdev and this larger group; it is their indifference toward the proclaiming of the virtues of their religion to others. Let's scrutinize for a moment the religious practices of a typical devotee within this tribe and see how they compare with those of Ramji.

For the sake of convenience, let's call this fellow Anthony. Our first contact with him convinces us that he is deeply religious. He is faithful to his ritual responsibilities and sensitive to spiritual values. His religion has made a commendable contribution toward his good way of life.

But let's listen to Anthony's prayers. His requests are woven around a tight little circle of loved ones and friends. They seldom reach beyond his localized situation and never—just never across the ocean. Obviously his god is a tribal deity.

Are sacrifices and offering a part of Anthony's worship? Indeed they are, and he is faithful in them. That is, as long as he can see some practical and personal benefit from them. If they will provide a more commodious place of worship for him, if they will lessen the amount of juvenile delinquency in his community and if they will provide schools where his children can become indoctrinated in his religion, then he is quite ready to give. In watching Anthony offer his sacrifices, one is convinced that the one who is the object of his worship is only interested in the local tribe.

It is already obvious to you that the tribe to which Anthony belongs is that large, gifted and God-blessed group of people called Christians. It is that group which has been chosen of God to be a witness of the grace of Christ to every tribe, race and nation. But Anthony, who is so typical of many in his tribe, seems as indifferent to a world without Christ as Ramji is to a world without Waghdev.

To Anthony God is bilingual, speaking only the language of heaven and English. God has no concern about getting the Gospel into other languages. God is nearsighted, seeing only the needs of men and women in the English-speaking world. God is limited in his capacity to

137

love and partial in his desire to receive worship. He is
provincial and nationalistic.

Get with It, Man,
Don W. Hillis, Moody, pages 22–25.

•••

It was that kind of obedience that prompted Tom and
Mary Mason to agree to house an international student
for the Memorial Day weekend in 1982. That was easy.
The pleasant Chinese graduate student from the nearby
University of Buffalo was a joy to meet. They fed him
breakfast, took him to church on Sunday, and had no
idea that encounter would change their lives.

Nothing much happened until the next year when
they agreed to help out again. Then the local director of
International Students asked Mary and her next-door
neighbor, Virginia, if they'd be willing to take a group of
Chinese students to Washington, D.C., for a week. Why
not? Neither one of the women had ever been to the
Capitol, and it sounded like an adventure. They had
only three days to prepare, so they sped to the AAA for
an itinerary, made lists and studied maps, and on a warm
July day, the two women, plus four children and seven-
teen students, headed down the New York thruway in
three vans.

"We literally did D.C. with a map in one hand while
pointing with the other," Mary laughs when she recalls
it. "We constantly got lost, but the Chinese joined in the

spirit of it and had a great time."

One afternoon—Mary had planned this—they stopped in the middle of the Mall between Washington Monument and the Lincoln Memorial and sat on the grass. Mary told the students how she had come to Jesus Christ and how He had changed her life. Then her daughter Beth played "Amazing Grace" on the violin while the students sang with them this song that was strange to them. It was a touching moment, although the students showed little response. That didn't surprise Mary. She had been told that characterized Orientals and she knew they were wary of being watched. One of them might have been—probably was—ready to report suspicious behavior to Beijing.

That fall, Mary and Virginia were invited to a Chinese dinner, a special occasion to celebrate the anniversary of the Cultural Revolution. Neither Mary nor Virginia knew before the dinner that they were the honored guests and the only Americans invited.

Toward the end of the evening, one of the Chinese women who had been on the trip to Washington pulled Mary aside and told her this story. "Do you see this little emblem I have on my lapel?" Mary nodded. It was an American flag. "Well," she said, "America will always be a special place for me. I thought about what you said in Washington and I accepted Jesus Christ as my Savior.

"I also decided I needed to make some changes in my life. I had come to this country to stay. We have been slowly getting our family out of China and only my

139

husband is left there. He is a high government official and can't leave yet. But now that I'm a Christian, my son has become a Christian, and we've decided to go home and share the Word with our family and our country."

"It was enough," says Mary, "to keep me going for years."

And keep going for years she has. The Masons began to host students for a week or two weeks at a time—mostly Japanese or Chinese. Then Mary began teaching English as a second language and holding Bible studies in her home. The latest was a Monday morning study made up of six Korean men and women.

One day when Gordon Loux visited the Masons, Tom hit the playback button on his telephone answering machine. A woman with a Japanese accent left a message that told it all: "Hi, Mom and Dad! Just called to say I love you. No need to call back."

The Masons will never know while on this earth how many lives they have influenced and in what way. That's true for most of us. Scrapbooks are crammed with stories of one person who got an idea or got mad or got unwittingly involved in a cause and ended up changing a community, or preserving the environment or saving lives.

You Can Be a Point of Light,
Gordon Loux and Ronald L. Wilson, Multnomah, pages
21–23.

CHAPTER SEVEN
MOVE WITH GOD
BEYOND YOUR
COMFORT ZONES

When I wake up I seldom remember what I've dreamed. People amaze men when they can recall not only what they've dreamed about, but the details as well.

In a similar fashion, when dreaming God's dreams, I sometimes find it hard to get them into sharp focus. That's because he doesn't always show me precisely what he has in mind. His dreams remain a bit fuzzy. Maybe that's the nature of dreams.

The Old Testament character Abraham knew what it was like to follow a divine dream without knowing all the details. God had promised that he would be the father of many nations, but as the years progressed, he passed the normal fathering age. Yet Abraham continued to believe the Dream Giver because he knew God is faithful. Later in Genesis we see the picture of this old man and his miracle son walking up Mt. Moriah to sacrifice to God. Once again, Abraham must have questioned how God's dream could be fulfilled if he sacrificed Isaac.

Another picture comes to mind from the New Testament, where people who heard God's call must have wondered what he was really asking of them. Recall the fishermen (Simon, Andrew, James, and John) leaving their nets because Jesus called to them, "Follow me . . . and I will make you fishers of men" (Matthew 4:19). But what did that challenge mean? It would take a lifetime for them to find out. Even so, what a privilege to begin dreaming God's dreams for them. That sure offered more sizzle than a lifetime spent in the fresh fish business.

Would you be excited if God said to you, "I have a dream I want you to share in"?

I'm sure that sounds good! And I don't want to discourage you. But this chapter underscores that those who accept God's invitation to dream his dreams usually have to break out of what I would call their "comfort zones." Such an invitation is extended to Thespia, a young actress in the book *Tales of the Resistance*. She is "the most beautiful player of all."

> The Dagoda of the Enchanter loomed in the middle of Enchanted City, so that none would forget the watching eye of the fire wizard. Close by, and a happier place was the Palace of Payers. Here the people of the city, filled with weariness and heartsickness, came and forgot for a time their griefs and fears and pains.
>
> Thespia stood in the wings of the stage brushing her long and luxuriant hair. She was the most beautiful of all the players and even now she could hear the house chanting her name. "Thespia! We want Thespia!" Many suitors sought her hand, but she turned then all away.

142

"Flowers from the Dagoda!" the assistant stage manager called. Thespia yawned and instructed that the gift be delivered to her suite in the Palace.

"Four minutes! Four minutes!" the callboy warned. Thespia straightened her gown and took one last look in the mirror.

Through a crack in the thick velvet curtain, she could see that the theater was full. It was almost time for the play to begin. *Poor ones. Poor, poor ones. Forget for a while, then home again only to remember your empty half-lives.* She whispered this hollow blessing over them.

"See you t'night," the lead actor shouted as he hurried to take his position. "QUIET!" warned the stage director.

"But . . ." Thespia wanted to protest to the actor; then she shrugged her shoulders and turned to wait for that always-thrill, the curtains rising and the stage filling with the sudden radiance of spotlights, then the sonorous voices of trained players. She particularly loved tonight's play. *The Return of the King* had been banned for years, but recently several very old myth cycles had been restored to the Palace repertoire.

We need a king—Thespia quickly looked around as though the stagehands could read her innermost mind. Treason, this thinking; she knew it. Careful, or the most beautiful player of all could play a final role tied to a stake at Burning Place. The first rule all children of Enchanted City learned after branding was:

THERE IS NO SUCH THING AS A KING.
DEATH TO PRETENDERS!

Senseless! she thought, and looked around again. If there's no such thing as a king, why such a fuss? The placards, the lectures, the propaganda songs— ". . . no king, no king, the Enchanter's the thi-ng." Silence

143

would have helped her to forget, but each protest made
her wish all the more: *If only there really were a king!*

I believe everyone dreams that dream. If only there
really were a king, a good and righteous king.

Certainly the destitute of the world hold to such a
dream. But then, I believe, so do the most beautiful of
entertainers, the most influential of leaders, even the
most wealthy and educated and acclaimed.

We are the ones who know there really is a King, aren't
we?

At one time, his dream for this world had first place in
our hearts. Now maybe the dream seems a bit fuzzy. It's
not as clear as it was before. Possibly other dreams have
crowded it out. We're not as willing to take the risks we
once took to see that dream fulfilled. We're older now,
more guarded.

"Three minutes! Three minutes!"

As a lonely understudy, Thespia had determined
to be the finest player in all Enchanted City. Unlike
the other actresses, who became arrogant and haughtily cut all ties with their pasts, Thespia perfected her
art in the streets. She refused to become enamored
with the sterile practice rooms, the posh living suites,
and the luxuries of the Palace of Players. She bound
up her flaxen hair with common cloth and walked
the marketplace, listening to how real people spoke
words.

Often she went back to her own people, to Moire
Oxan where they lived, to the stacked hovels where

144

she had been raised. There she carried old grannys' burdens that weighed their bent backs double and she brought tidbits of food for the always-hungry waifs. She wept when orphans were taken away to the Orphan Keeper and she felt the cold whistling through these always night lives, and remembered what it was to never have enough fire or power.

Their pain became her own, and their small and meagre joys as well. Because she did not despise them, she was loved: and it was they, the street people sitting on the gallery floor, who called her name.

One night, one terrible night, her cousin's wee babe wriggled in agony in Thespia's arms while searchers hunted its mother who was foraging in a city-edge workshift. It squinched up its tiny face, took a last, long breath, and died. Shuddering with sobs, Thespia hid in a tower of the Players' Palace. How could she act the next night, play the comic, with this terrible knowledge—that babies died who shouldn't die in Enchanted City. She grieved with new understanding—there was little she, or anyone, could do.

Another young woman we know of probably had similar feelings about there being little she could do to alleviate the misery and suffering surrounding her. The powerful Romans had conquered her nation and that meant life was rough on everyone. *So just try not to make trouble, and exercise caution where you go, especially if you're young and attractive.*

Spiritually sensitive, one thing wonderful was that Mary was engaged to a just and good man who, would you believe, was a descendant of Israel's great King David. Undoubtedly, this relationship was seen as a gift from God and represented Mary's greatest security.

BREAKING OUT OF YOUR COMFORT ZONE

Be careful, however, not to hold too tightly to what you have. Keep it in an open palm, Mary. As wonderful as your love for Joseph seems, the Lord has a greater role for you to fill. It will eclipse everything you have known so far. You're to play a critically important part in the coming of the Messiah, God's anointed King, the Son of the Most High. So hold on to everything rather lightly—the upcoming marriage, the future family plans, the small home you plan to set up, the friends and security you know in this village.

These elements might have represented Mary's comfort zone.

What's yours?

> Your position?
> Your salary?
> Your business?
> Your house?
> Your family?
> Your friendships?
> Your parents' approval?
> Your good life?
> Your attractive appearance?
> Your retirement package?

Your investments?
Your recognition?
Your title?

What represents for you what the engagement, the wedding talk, the friends in the home town, and the protection of a respected husband meant for Mary—or what the stage lights, the costumes, the applause, the leading roles symbolized for Thespia?

Do you know?

Let me warn you not to hold onto such items too tightly. Don't close your fingers around them. Instead, display these items on an open palm.

You see, the real King might soon be saying, "I have a dream I want you to share in. Does that sound good to you? And do you think, if necessary, you could break out of your comfort zone? Could you put all you have in my hands?"

After the dramatic encounter with Gabriel, Mary needed to talk with someone. Normally, that would have been Joseph. But telling him what the angel said to her would have been difficult, especially the part about, "The Holy Spirit will come upon you, and the power of the Most High will overshadow you" (Luke 1:35). Had she even remembered correctly what was told her? It was certainly a thrilling message, yet at the same time it must have been somewhat terrifying.

The three-month visit with her cousin Elizabeth was reassuring, but it didn't solve all of Mary's problems. We

147

know that when she returned home Joseph was deeply troubled by the fact that she was expecting.

Pssst, Mary—get used to God nudging you out of your comfort zone. The role he's fashioned for you demands it.

Now, listen carefully to wrinkly old Simeon's words when you take your infant son to be presented as the Law requires. Yes, this elderly gentleman is thrilled to see with his own eyes the Savior God has promised. So thrilled that now he can die in peace! But those last words he says, does he have to say that? "And a sword will pierce your very soul" (Luke 2:35, NLT).

Herod's hired assassins didn't put a sword through the baby Jesus or his mother. But they destroyed the lives of "all the boys in and around Bethlehem who were two years old and under" (Matthew 2:16, NLT). News of that traumatic event must have been unnerving.

Mary also missed out on the hometown surroundings of friends and family up in Nazareth. Instead, it was a hurried flight in the night to Egypt for the young mother, adopted father, and toddler. Here they would stay until murderous King Herod finally departed the scene.

The immense responsibility of knowing she was secretly raising the future King, who had been promised her people through the centuries, must at times have been overwhelming for Mary. We get a hint of this ongoing tension when the couple lost track of Jesus in Jerusalem. He was twelve years old. "Why have you done this to us?" questioned Mary. "Your father and I have been frantic, searching for you everywhere!" (Luke 2:48, NLT).

148

Can you hear the stress in her voice?

As Jesus reached maturity, it's possible his mother prodded her son a bit to get about doing what he was supposed to do and revealing his true identity. Is this what happened at the wedding in Cana? "My time has not yet come," he told her (John 2:4).

The eventual popularity of her firstborn must have pleased Mary. His message about his kingship or kingdom was clear and compelling, but also a bit bold and dangerous if Romans were in the crowd. It was hard for her to get an accurate reading on what the people were thinking. Apparently there were even times of conflict with family members regarding what was happening. Once they even tried to take Jesus home, stating, "He's out of his mind" (Mark 3:21).

"We know who your father is!" said the religious leaders to Jesus derisively (John 8:19). It was a slam Mary would hear about more than once in her life.

Nothing was as difficult, however, as the wrenching experience of Calvary where our Lord's mother watched her son die a horribly painful death—and in many ways, the scene made absolutely no sense to her.

So, would this remarkable woman be up to the stretching assignment that wouldn't really end until she died? "Confused and disturbed" is what the Bible says she was during the initial visit from Gabriel (Luke 1:29, NLT). After a good number of years like this had passed, would Mary still be willing to say, "I am the Lord's servant, and I am willing to accept whatever he wants" (v. 38)?

149

Let's face it. Hers was hardly a comfortable life. So often we learn from Scripture that to be a part of God's dreams for us we must become spiritual risk-takers. We have to break out of our comfort zones. We need to dare to dream in ways we had never imagined.

As the life assignment you have been given by God unfolds, have you put your hand up and said, "Stop. I've had enough. You're pushing me too much. Maybe you didn't notice, but my heels are dug in. Now leave me alone, please!" Or are you a Mary, who trusts God and says, "I'm your trusting servant, Lord. I'm willing to accept whatever you want for me"?

I'd suggest once again that you figure out what represents your comfort zone. Get an actual picture of it that you can put in your Bible. The bank account, the new home, the family, the position. For me it's my calendar, my daily planner. That may not make much sense to you, but with all my deadlines I find that my life is almost slave to a schedule. If the Holy Spirit has a message for me, it's almost as if my response is, "I can talk Thursday at 2:00, Lord. How's that?"

So my comfort zone picture is a sheet from my calendar. This is the entrapment from which I have to break free. I put the calendar sheet in my Bible so that the Scriptures can stretch me. Have you noticed they do this if we let them, if our comfort zones don't crowd out what the Lord wants to say to us through his Word?

Well, Thespia, the most beautiful player of all, was open to the young King's moving her out of her comfort zone. Let's return to that story. The play, *The Return of the King,* has begun.

"P-s-s-s-t, Thespia," the prompter hissed. "Entrance!"

She stepped onto the stage, her hair tumbling in captured stagelight, glowing like a halo. There was a gasp from the gallery and applause from the boxes. She closed her eyes and evoked the memory of the roseate sun, rising, rising—and stood shimmering beneath the overhead spotlights. "Oh, we are mortals and have forgotten how to laugh. Who will show us where laughter is hiding?" Thespia's lashes glistened with tears because it was true, so true.

Perhaps Thespia's power came from the gallery, from the men and women and children sitting on the floor and wearing ragged, tattered clothes. They, too, wondered where the laughter had gone. Most players acted to the boxes, to the rich patrons dripping with furs, sitting in plush chairs, their stomachs full. But Thespia played to the floor, to the people. She looked at them with pity. Eager, the whole mob lifted their heads to the stagelight, their mouths open, their eyes wide with wonder.

Thespia loved to make them laugh, loved their unsophisticated whooping, howling, and floor pounding. She loved to make them weep, to spill the overflow of sorrow that became dammed in the dark horrors of Enchanted City.

Tonight beyond the circle of reflected stagelight, she thought she saw a man standing, but he was in the gallery shadow. *Strange. Why don't the ushers have him sit or leave?*

Two stage beats, a pause. At this moment, the

actor/king stepped from the wing. This was one of the play's dramatic moments, the actual return of the King; but suddenly, the lights flickered and dimmed. A groan went up from the theater.

"Power out! Oh-h-h-h-h-h. Power out!"

Even the players on stage moaned.

"Lights! Lights! Lights!" shouted the street people.

"Doesn't anything ever work in this wretched city!" In dismay Thespia realized she had spoken out loud. The actor/king leaned close to her, "*Careful!* Rumors say there's revolt underfoot."

But then Thespia realized that a light *was* shining in the darkened auditorium. The man she had seen in the gallery shadow seemed to be standing in his own light. She gasped and took a closer look; he seemed vaguely familiar. From the back of the hall, he raised his hand in greeting. Shyly, hardly realizing she did so, she reached out her hand toward him.

And the theater quieted as all watched the man walk within a center of radiance to the orchestra pit. He perched upon the rim, apologized to the musicians, and vaulted up to the stage. "This is where I make my entrance, I believe," he said, and his voice was wonderful, filled with the echo of faraway hills and laughing country streams.

He stood in the middle of the stage and held out strong arms. "There is a real kingdom," he announced, "and a real king."

Without knowing that they moved, all the players took one step closer to his warmth. Some in the gallery rose to their knees.

The man motioned to the conductor. "Music," he said, and the orchestra began to play. "Up tempo." The beat quickened in the percussion section and

wound its way in and out among the street people
whose feet began to tap.

"In the Kingdom of Light, there is no night."

And the man smiled at the gallery, at all in the
house and at the players onstage. The beat waltzed its
way to the tiers of boxes, and even a few of the
wealthy patrons began to clap: *Ta-dum-ta-dum-ta-da-da-dum.*

"In the Kingdom of Light," the man chanted, "the
day shines bright."

The music was infectious. Now many chanted
back, "In the Kingdom of Light, the day shines
bright."

Ta-da-ta-da-ta-da-da-dum, played the orchestra.
The man raised his hands for quieter music.

"Have you ever heard of a kingdom where outcasts
were welcomed?" the man asked.

And the people answered, "No-o-o-o-o!"

"Have you ever heard of a kingdom where every
orphan had a home?"

"No-o-o-o-o-o-o-o-o!"

"Or where those who loved light could live in it?
Or where those who sought for a king found him?"

The man lowered his voice to a stage whisper, and
the whole audience leaned forward to hear, "In the
Kingdom of Light, everything's right!"

Ah-h-h-h-h-h-h-h, sighed the house. And for a
moment, everyone in the audience knew this man
was no play, no myth cycle dragged out of the palace
archives. *"Ah-h-h-h-h-h-h-h,"* sighed the gallery again,
a long sigh. If only there were such a place, such a
real place.

The man offered his arm to the actor-king standing on one side of him and his other arm to Thespia

153

who also stood near. She looked out on the audience and gasped—the people in the gallery were clothed in warm garments, their runny sores were healed, they were clean and healthy. This couldn't be true. She blinked her eyes and stared again and realized she was seeing the people through the glow of the man's light.

Tears ran down her cheeks, real tears, not player's tears. If it could only be; if there really were such a place. "Wh-wh-who are you?" she asked, and he answered, "You know who I am." Sobs broke her words, "But h-how do w-we find this kingdom of w-which you speak?"

He turned, took both her hands in one hand, and wiped away her tears. The other players gathered close, and one put his arm around Thespia's shoulders to comfort her.

"Follow me," said the man. "The real kingdom is wherever I walk and whenever anyone walks with me."

Thespia knew. He was wearing common clothes, the plain garments of the people, but she wanted to fall at his feet and bow. Tears blurring her vision, she turned from the man, faced the audience, and walked to the edge of the stage. She stretched one hand to him and one hand to the gallery, as if in introduction. "The King," she said. "My Lord, the people."

Suddenly, the lights blinked off-on; the man-made power was coming up. Someone in the boxes shouted: THERE IS NO SUCH THING AS A KING! DEATH TO PRETENDERS! And several began to chant: DEATH! DEATH!

The orchestra stopped playing and all the notes

154

tumbled together and fell in a heap, and the man-made power suddenly came fully on and the lights blazed forth. The audience shifted in their seats and patted their clothes straight. What a strange play—it must be intermission—but then all those old myth cycles were odd. They stood to stretch. And the magical moment was gone and the players exited, trying to remember what lines had been said and which lines remained to be said and who had the last cue; and the stage director didn't know which act to call next.

I have prayed even as I've been putting this chapter together that this might be a magical spiritual moment for you. It's never too late to dream.

"Follow me," said Jesus to the fishermen in the gospels, and they left their nets. Their response was like that of Abraham in the Old Testament. He stepped out in faith because God said, "I have a new place where I want you to move. Can you leave the comfort of where you are?"

Do you recall the angel Gabriel's words? "Don't be frightened, Mary, . . . for God has decided to bless you!" (Luke 1:30, NLT). The Lord was about to do something wonderful through her that would bless all generations across the entire world. Don't miss this unique opportunity—don't opt for the comfort zone.

• Be more vocal in your witness.

• Say, "Lord, as your steward, I acknowledge that the

155

money, the savings—they're really yours."

• Pray, "God, if you have a new assignment for me, I'm ready."

• Be willing to break a glass ceiling if doing so makes for entry into a new world.

The Scriptures can come alive for you again! Realize that to dream God's dreams, all of us must overcome barriers that hold us back, including inappropriate comfort zones. Let your response to the King be like that of Thespia.

Thespia stayed beside the man, who was buttoning his coat as though he meant to go. "Are you leaving?" she asked.

"Yes, the moment for believing is gone."

She held her breath. "C-can I come with you?"

He bowed and took her hand and kissed it; then he helped her climb as gracefully as possible over the orchestra pit, and they walked down the aisle and left the theatre together. And very few seemed to see them go.

And Thespia became a street player in the back alleys and dead ends of Enchanted City, acting out the King's story in such a way that all who saw her suspected— then hoped—that there was a real kingdom. Like the King, she worked in common clothes, and she never gave the luxuries of the Palace a backward glance, because when one has found one's real love it is easy to leave what has only been pretend.

FOR DISCUSSION AND REFLECTION

1. What are some unhealthy comfort zones Christians sometimes settle into?

2. Tell about someone you know who risked breaking out of comfortable confines.

3. When in the past have you broken through a similar barrier?

4. What are ways you presently see yourself responding to God's gentle nudgings?

5. Name the fears that haunt you when you think about what God wants you to do.

6. What safeguards are there to keep spiritual risk-taking from getting out of hand?

Readings

But I do not so easily return to the fray when I've been intimidated. I do not automatically walk back into the fire when I've been burned. My instinct is to go where the environment is cordial, warm, and affirming. Left to my feelings, I will avoid the conflict—stay out of the community when I've been threatened, choose another class when I've been attacked by the professor. My natural response is to protect my emotional comfort.

But God calls me not to emotional comfort but to obedience. I am to drive back through the woods where drunken men point guns in my face, not out of feeling but out of conviction, not because of the heart but because of the head. Risk is never a matter of the heart; it's always a matter of the will. I do not risk because I feel like it. I risk because of what God wants me to do.

But my head does not so easily take control. I am a rational creature, yes, but I am also created with glands and hormones, palms that sweat in fear and muscles that tighten in anger. What do I do with the emotional side of my nature? How do I rise above it and free myself for risk?

If I would know risk, I must confront the two sides of myself that fight for dominance. My feelings tell me to stay away from Blairston and his oral interpretation course. My reason says to complete the quarter. There

158

are only six more weeks. I must decide whether reason or feelings will rule. If I follow feelings, where will they lead me? I will get an incomplete and will have wasted the entire quarter. Where will following my reason lead? To restoration with Dr. Blairston, at least on my part. To a grade. To the satisfied feeling that I did not run from a tough situation.

If I would learn to risk emotional discomfort, sometimes, away from the heat of the moment, I may need to stop and take a more general inventory. Do feelings or reason dictate the majority of my responses? Are my feelings keeping me from doing things I need to do, things I believe God would have me do? Is hospitable environment more important than obedience? Comfort more important than conviction?

If I would know risk, conviction must always be my criterion. I must obey whether I feel like it or not. I must drive through the woods even when I am scared. I must face Dr. Blairston even when I've been humiliated by him.

If I would know risk, I must be willing to walk without receiving positive emotional strokes from those around me. I must be willing to be unpopular with certain people, unwelcome in certain places. With Jesus, I must follow the dusty roads of Galilee toward Jerusalem, even though I know the cross awaits me there—the ultimate unwelcome.

Beyond Safe Places,
Ruth Senter, Harold Shaw, pages 94–96.

Only 4 out of 10 pastors claim their church is completely or mostly open to new styles of ministry. A number of pastors expressed disappointment that their people are unwilling to experiment with new formats for ministry or are unwilling to take risks in the development of new programs, strategies and activities.

"Creatively, I feel stifled," bemoaned one minister. "People always resist change, but it seems that within the church we major on trying to retain what we've always done just so we won't have to take a chance. I'm quite concerned that this mentality is spreading and can only impair our ability as individuals and as a community to grow."

The resistance to new styles was most keenly felt by pastors of small churches. Whereas 6 out of 10 pastors of larger churches felt the freedom to try new things, only 1 out of 3 pastors in churches of fewer than 50 people felt the same sense of liberty.

Today's Pastors,
George Barna, Regal, page 88

•••

Letting go of possessions breaks the bonds of comfort. But if I want to be freed all the way, in the biblical sense, if I want to go beyond giving up what isn't needed, the next step is for me to prayerfully listen to my conscience, then to take risks. Not just any risks, but the risks that God demands.

Sometimes we are too safe to be alive. Stripping one-self of wealth takes away the numbness only for a while, if the soul is not transformed. For wealth itself is not the problem. It's my attitude—an attitude of fear that makes me protect myself excessively, that demands comfort. It's that attitude that determines whether or not I stay trapped inside the cocoon, trapped in soft and sleepy blindness. And when that protective attitude stands in the way, there's nothing that can substitute for simply *doing the difficult thing.*

It may be as small as stopping to help a stranger stranded on the highway. It may be driving into the city one night a week and parking in a rough neighborhood so I can serve at a soup kitchen. It may be even larger—taking in a rent-free boarder who needs a safe home, changing my job, adopting a child. These risks, made with such effort, will wrench me back into reality. They are like fresh air introduced into a garage full of carbon monoxide.

Without listening to God, I do not know what is truly healthy for myself. Risking for risk's sake is not the answer. But risking for God's sake is. And God is always wanting us to risk for his sake, just as his Son Jesus did. Thankfully, he knows that taking such risks is difficult, and he will not ask more than we can give.

On a flight out of Ethiopia several years ago, I met a gentle, kind-spirited man who took unusual interest in my wife and me. He seemed delighted to meet us and he was curious to know our stories, as well as to share his own. He turned out to be chairman for the board of a major relief-and-development organization.

Hamilton was there with a film crew, making a documentary on hunger in East Africa. In fact, as I learned from a crew member, he had paid for most of the filming out of his own pocket. During our conversation, he admitted reluctantly that he was an attorney by trade. For years he had made his living (and apparently a very good one at that) by doing legal work, but he had never found satisfaction in it. Then he became involved with relief-and-development work.

"For the first time, I felt as if my life had meaning," he said, laughing sheepishly. "I mean that. As an attorney, you've got to wonder sometimes if you have any meaning at all."

In my opinion, Hamilton showed that he had broken out of the shell of comfort. No person enslaved to security would have risked going into Ethiopia at that time—when Eritrean rebels had pushed within eighty miles of Addis Ababa and when Colonel Mengistu was rumored to be on the verge of toppling from power. Nor would he have traveled into the destitute areas where this film crew had to work, risking the diseases that rage through. But Hamilton had, and as a result he was spiritually alive. He had been set free from the illusion that his comfort, like Aling Nena's Virgin Mary, would somehow magically make life livable, worthwhile. To him, it was a delight that people around the world were coming to

Christ because they saw Christians like himself giving of their wealth and risking involvement, no matter how stressful or dangerous that might be.

Hamilton was unusual. He had the strength to become spiritually alive while staying wealthy. Most do not have that strength. Saint Francis, for one, knew that he needed to break from wealth altogether. He literally stripped the clothes off his body so that they would not stand between him and God. He did not want any comfort if it meant captivity.

But Francis was rewarded for his action with riches beyond compare, for in taking that step he learned the truth stated so well by Thomas à Kempis, a monk who lived only one hundred years later, in the fourteenth century: "O my soul, thou can'st not be fully comforted, nor have perfect refreshment, except in God, the Comforter of the poor, and Patron of the humble."

Each of us needs to be set free from comfort. We need to ask, How much do I really need? Any more can become a trap. And to prove our willingness to live with less, we need to take the risks that God asks of us. There is wonderful liberation in letting go.

The Comfort Trap,
Tim Bascom, InterVarsity, pages 58–60.

CHAPTER EIGHT
BELIEVE THAT WITH GOD ALL THINGS ARE POSSIBLE

If you had been a heavenly advisor to Jesus, would you have recommended that he go ahead with his plan to take on human flesh? Perhaps you would have cautioned him, "You've already done everything imaginable, Your Majesty. You've been repeatedly rejected by humans. How many more times do you need to be hurt by them? Don't do it!"

Fortunately for us, Jesus was willing to leave the security and comforts of heaven and lower himself to our station in life so we could know restoration and a proper relationship with God. The dream of close fellowship with those he made was not abandoned, and at the proper time, our Lord was born of the Virgin Mary.

It's mind-boggling when you think about it. What an amazing heart of love is revealed by Christ's actions! The saying remains true: With God all things are possible.

From the time he began his ministry here on earth, Jesus fired people's imaginations with a dream of what could be. His visionary presentation was about a new kind of kingdom, or kingship. Christ was saying that for people to know a better world, they needed to willingly recognize him as their rightful leader, or king. Wherever he went, he talked about this kingship, or kingdom. In a most appealing manner, he said that it was to the advantage of his hearers to buy into what he was offering.

"The leaders you have now—when you're in deep sorrow, when you mourn, do they comfort you? Is that what Herod does? No. But you're blessed, my friends, because now you can come under my rule. Under my kingship, those who mourn are comforted. Watch how I live among you. My way of life verifies what I'm telling you.

"Listen to me. This is good news! Do you hunger and thirst for righteousness, for what's right in the eyes of God? In Pilate's hall of judgment, is that where you expect to find righteousness? You know better. But under my kingship, you'll discover what you're looking for. I'll show you what's right in God's eyes. When I'm on the throne, you'll be satisfied and blessed.

"You who are meek—yes, you, and you, ma'am—is it to your advantage to be meek under Caesar? Not really, But under my reign, it's the meek—yes, you—who will inherit the earth."

Christ's kingdom talk was electrifying! The Jewish population longed for the revealing of the anointed one of God, the great Jewish king who had been promised, their Messiah. That's what the word *Messiah* means, "the anointed of God." The word *Christ* means the same thing. It's Greek for "the anointed one." *Christ* and *Messiah* are synonyms. One is a Greek word; the other is Hebrew. If I say Jesus Christ, that means the same as Jesus Messiah, Jesus the anointed one.

ANTI-ESTABLISHMENT

For some years the little country of Israel had been buzzing with Messiah talk. Stories had been circulating for twenty to thirty years about a miracle child whom King Herod had tried to kill, but who had escaped unharmed.

This kind of Messiah talk always made the Roman forces edgy, even with their overwhelming military superiority.

I'm sure the Jewish leadership of the time saw this newcomer, Jesus, as youthful. They probably did not appreciate his criticism of their traditional values. In fact, over the months and years, the young Jesus became increasingly dangerous in the minds of the establishment.

But they couldn't articulate an alternative vision that captured the fancy of the people. Yes, they had a power, of sorts, but there was no longer any magic in their words. They knew they were no match for Christ, especially when he demonstrated supernatural powers.

For the Sanhedrin (the Jewish high court) to affirm his message would require changes few in their ranks were willing to make. Their bottom line, wealth, seemed to have little meaning to Jesus. What mattered to him was love—love for God and love for others. Treating people the way you wanted them to treat you was what he advocated.

In a way, Jesus was a bit of a comic figure to the leaders of his day. He seemed so naïve, so idealistic, so ignorant of politics and power. "Treat others the way you want them to treat you." Anybody with the least amount of sense could figure out in an instant how to take advantage of that philosophy. This was especially true of the Romans.

There are eras when nothing changes, no matter what. Then there are times when change is in the air. You can sense it coming; it appears inevitable. This was one of those times.

What would happen? Obviously, the Jewish religious system wasn't working well, except for the pious few.

Good or bad, it wasn't long before the Jewish Council members knew that Jesus was walking a different path than they were. By Passover of his final year, it looked as if the crowds were following him. They were crying, "Blessed is the king who comes in the name of the Lord!" (Luke 19:38).

Even a few months back, who would have thought this possible? It made the religious leaders nervous. They would have to do all they could to defeat him before the groundswell became too great to stop.

I really like this King Jesus I see in the Scriptures. He was one of a kind! For someone in his early thirties, he showed remarkable maturity. Unfortunately, it's hard to describe Jesus in fresh terms. So much has been written about him. These words from *Tales of the Resistance* describe a fictional king. They might give us a fitting picture of King Jesus as well.

> Thespia had fallen hopelessly in love with the King. Oh, not the actor/king (though he was handsome and her ardent admirer), but the mythical king of the play—the one who was strong but not brutal, who could laugh with joy and weep with freedom, who never leered at beautiful women, who told stories to children and gentled the fears of the old, whom the young men followed because he was the bravest of all, who found beauty in the ugly, and whose very words spoke hope.

Like Thespia, I too love this young King. I like the man, and I like his plan—his dream for the world.

I believe that if we all lived as he did, if we all said, "Jesus, your thoughts will be my thoughts. Your ways, Jesus, will be my ways. Your rule, Jesus, the rule I swear allegiance to above all else"—this sad world would become a most wonderful place almost overnight. We would know the joy of having food for all, dignity for all, peace over all. In fact, I don't think there's any other way to make the world work. I really don't!

You love this King too, don't you?

THE BEST DIED YOUNG

The world shouldn't kill its good men and women. Dreamers are too rare to begin with. But sometimes the world destroys its best.

169

Jimmy Carter was a national leader and a man of noble dreams. He still is. If we heard that authorities somewhere had arrested him and beaten him in Rodney King fashion, and in the process of carrying out supposed justice they had killed him, we would be shocked. "What has the world come to?" we would ask.

When Gallup pollsters ask who are the most admired men and women, what names are predictable?

- Billy Graham
- The pope
- President Bush and his wife, Laura
- Colin Powell

Let them all live to old age. Don't kill the good ones off.

Thank goodness there were no headlines 20 or 30 years ago declaring, "Billy Graham Shot and Killed While Sharing God's Good News"! While attempts of deranged individuals or hired assassins fail and the pope lives or our president is only wounded, I thank the Lord.

Yet, how can it be that in the long history of the world, the finest of all persons would be arrested as a young man and roughed up and tried and spit upon and convicted of blasphemy by the Jewish high court? How could Herod and Pilate remove themselves from the process of justice and say to a hired crowd, "I've whipped him senseless. Isn't that enough for you? All right, then, what you do to him next is your responsibility, not mine."

Have I reached past your mind to your feelings yet?

That's what I'm attempting to do.

Fiction has a way of putting us in touch with our emotions and giving us new insights. Like C. S. Lewis in *The Lion, the Witch and the Wardrobe,* a fiction writer says, in essence, "Let me take you to another world. If you can see what's happening there, maybe you can better comprehend what takes place in your own world." Let's return to Enchanted City, where Amanda, another young woman who loves the King, has sneaked into the court to observe his trial. All seems discouraging and unfair and hopeless and heavy.

> "First witness," cried the Clerk.
>
> It was the Chief Herald, the one formerly known as Doublespeak. His friends said that he was Doublespeak no more, but Doomster, the one who pronounced judgment for the Enchanter. The emblem of the fire wizard was emblazoned on his elegant purple jersey; he wore brass armbands and a circlet of gold upon his head. "Why, I heard, I heard with my very own ears this man, this prisoner there, proclaim another kingdom, where the subjects live in the light. He attempted to entice me, me, the Chief Herald to the Enchanter, to treason."
>
> Someone in the courtroom called out, "Treachery!" Another shouted, "Death to pretenders!"
>
> The Clerk banged his gavel for order. The man in the center of the courtroom spoke not a word.
>
> Amanda studied him carefully. His shoulders sagged as though he was suffering great sorrow. He seemed drawn within himself—the proceedings in

171

that place made no difference. It was as though he had walked into a great aloneness and was not even present.

Seeing! thought Amanda. If she could see into the King's mind. Closing her eyes, Amanda aimed her gifts at the great soul of the man standing in disguise before her. A wave of enormous sadness overcame her. Tears began to stream down her cheeks and she was tempted to withdraw her sight. *"Nay-nay-nay,"* intoned the song of doom. The King's mind was entering into every dark place in Enchanted City— no, more—taking all the darkness into his very center.

Amanda could see nothing. The dark blindness overwhelmed her, but somehow she realized that her sight labored by the side of her dear King, the one she loved most in all the world.

"My Liege Lord," she whispered in her heart, and the man in front of her stirred slightly, as though he had heard and recognized her words with his own soul. It was then Amanda realized that nothing could be done, that for now, there was no light in the King, that he had for some reason of his own knowing joined with this deepest and most impenetrable darkness.

Through him Amanda stared into the shadow of death itself, into the night of all nights that begins and has no ending, and she withdrew, opening her eyes, unable to bear any more the grimacing features of total despair.

It was then she saw them, circling the rim of the courtyard, standing beyond and above and over the Burners and Breakers: gorgeous, brilliant, shining— the Bright Ones! They were translucent, shimmering.

172

As Amanda glanced quickly at the miserable creatures sitting on benches, cold, shivering with fear,
hopeless, glad for one wretched moment of reprieve
at the expense of the most beautiful man who ever
lived, the princess realized that no one else was aware
of these creatures of indescribable glory.

Unknowing, they were all surrounded by these
exquisite, unseen beings who glistened like raindrops
on cobwebs blown by the wind, who turned like gos-
samer milkpod seeds in the brilliant sunlight, who
raised their eyes filled with star glory, and stretched
their wings, tip to tip, now gold, now silver, now
pure light on light. The Bright Ones bent their
graces toward the man in the center of this trial, pre-
venting any interruption of purpose from breaking
his intense concentration.

Their looks focused on the King in the center,
holding off tenderness, staying any loving-kindness
lest goodness distract him from the work of breaking
the Enchanter's spell, which held all the city in its
grip. They were not helping him; they were only
keeping him from being interrupted. Amanda could
see that they, too, wept.

The Princess turned her moist and opened eyes to
the King. Now she understood that he was deliber-
ately restraining his own power. He was not defeated
by the gathering evil oppression in the hold of the
fire wizard. The King was holding himself in, con-
taining command and nobility, silencing his majestic
authority, confining his royalty in order to descend
by the way of mind and spirit into the center of dark
agony, the very secret evil crux of the Enchanter's
domain. He was preparing himself to be the willing
victim who would lift the enchantment from the
city.

173

It was then Amanda realized that the trial had gone on, that other witnesses had been called, that now the courtroom was a chaos of noise. "Burn him! Burn him!" the people screamed. "Death to the pretender!" pronounced the Chief Herald.

"TO THE BURNING PLACE!" screamed the Enchanter, and the iron cauldrons flared orange at the pronouncement of sentence. The death drums rolled. The pokers of the Burners glowed. The fire wizard removed his black robe of condemnation. The gavel pounded, raising sparks.

Amanda's heart broke at this judgment and she sobbed aloud, no longer hiding herself. For once it made no matter, for the evil eye sought only one victim, one sacrificial captive, and that One remained still, silent in the rising riot as the Enchanter began for procession of death.

So the Enchanter's men came a last time and took into custody the One who could walk into the center of madness, who could make his way into the underworld of each child's life, whose very name freed the prisoner, whose promise of a Kingdom made life worth playing, who brought light into all dark places. The One who could sing the whole song, who could call each orphan by name. The only One who could stare the Enchanter in the eye, who could challenge the very dominion of evil. The One who begins the dance of celebration again at life's end—the King, the true King.

When someone you deeply love is suddenly killed, it leaves you stunned.

When that death is a violent one, and the person's body is mutilated, you feel even worse.

- "I just saw him alive and well, smiling and waving to the crowds. It was on TV—he was in a convertible driving through downtown Dallas. Jackie was there by his side. Then there were these shots from somewhere. Apparently a couple of bullets just tore his head open."

- "World leaders waving to the crowds—where was it? The Summit in Paris, or the Passover celebration in Jerusalem? When was that? Just last week, wasn't it? Yes, he smiled and waved, beautiful smile. Now he's dead?"

When torture is involved, friends feel violated themselves, physically sick, deeply disturbed, confused.

- "He must have been the most wonderful leader the world has ever known, the person who had the most amazing ideas, the most thrilling of dreams. It's a tragedy—what a loss. Who could possibly ever replace him?"

A torch is lit. The priest touches it to the pyre. The flames burst into the night. They whoosh; they burn; they leap higher and higher. The wild wind roars, feeding the conflagration. The shadow at the stake lifts, arches, raises its head, and is crowned with burning.

The Enchanter is a writhing, frenzied silhouette before the fire. He lifts his distorted face to the flames, "Owa-ha-ha! Owa-ha-ha!"—the howl of a beast over its prey. OWA-HA-HA! OWA-HA-HA!

But each common man stands pierced to the soul, watching the crackling flames, the leaping cinders, the

175

chorus of fire singing raucously upon the pyre. For all know now, though they may forget it tomorrow: the wizard will feel joy at any burning place, at any death time, at any agony of final passing. He will preside in gleeful dance at any dying. . .

A beautiful woman with flaxen hair falls to her knees in the ash dust. Will she never again act out stories in the streets? . . . Will she nevermore speak the rhymes of peace, the poetry of hope, the prose of power? Will the memory of the tale be broken, the most wonderful story of all be locked away in the archives, never to be retold? . . .

In the darkness, a crowd begins to gather, a throng—all those who have loved and served the King, all those who have worked in the resistance; each man, woman, and child who ever dared to believe in the breaking of enchantments or dared to hope in a future restoration. All who longed for the exile to end now stand mourning in the ashes of the death of all dreams and try to remember light, and song, and life.

The Keeper of the Chronicle of Sightings of the King stands silent, too, stripped of hope, ravaged. The Enchanter is the victor after all, death his second-in-command. *There is no such thing as a Kingdom,* he thinks. *Great Park is only make-believe. . . I am no Hero, nor a King's man. The city saying is so: "There is no such thing as a King." This is and will ever be the keep of the Great Enchanter.*

He holds the handle of the hatchet by his side, feeling no power. *We have tricked ourselves,* he thinks and casts the tool to the ground. Then he sits in the ashes, his heart too much of stone for weeping.

He stares at the gathering crowd, shadows in the

blackness. *Why are they here? It's all over. We all are orphans, all ugly deformed scarboys, sewer rats and boiler brats, carnival girls, heralds of untruths.* And we must all return to Enchanted City, this place of the no-people. The time for heroics is ended.

He sits motionless; he sleeps but sees no visions. Numb, he rests not. He wakes to darkness; no day comes. Will this night never end? All is done. Over. Never to be again, a forever unhappiness.

In the night, he thinks that the shadows, forms deeper than the substance of darkness, creep closer to the pyre which rises black, a rubble of twisted cinder and charcoal, in the middle of Burning Place. Someone stands beside him, and reaches to him a hand. It is an old, old woman, more bent than ever, the grasp now feeble. It is Mercie.

"Why are they here?" he asks her, motioning to the shadows. "Must all who love him come?"

Her voice is weak; her answer sounds far away. "Yes. All who love the King must come to this place before they can see the Restoration begin."

He wants to scoff. He wants to shout silence, but his eye is caught by a tiny glow on the pyre—*embers that are not completely burned.* Others in the gathered congregation of shadows see it, too; they gasp. Peering, he rises to his knees, but wait! The glow suddenly becomes a flame, one small warm ring of light, not an angry destroying rage, but a good burning, a flower flame, growing strangely larger and larger, unfolding upon itself, petals of soft fire, layer upon layer opening outward, white, rose, golden, glowing.

In this sudden light, he can see that the shadows are the people of Great Park who have stood in the

177

darkness, waiting, waiting. Here a band of Rangers in forest garb. There orphans newly arrived, their faces scrubbed but filled with anxiety. He spies Amanda. This has been a night of anguish for her; her face is haggard, but her eyes—they seem to be filled with sight. And beyond them all, strange forms of soft, almost indistinguishable luminescence.

As the flower of fire grows, he sees his comrades from the taxi resistance, people of the city, brave men and women whose faces are now filling with wonder. Nearby stands Caretaker, his back straightening in the warmth of the new flame.

Then out of the center of the lovely burning light, a laugh! His heart leaps. He has heard that laugh before. His being lurches with hope.

It is the laugh of the King!

All stare into the middle of the death field, into the flaming flower, their mouths agape, their eyes open wide. A form is taking shape in the middle of the pistils and the stamen. A real form is rising from the burning center. It gathers unto itself, becoming distinct, definite, firm. The watchers narrow their vision in order to see better what they can scarcely believe they are seeing. It's the King—the King! He stands tall, stands bold. He stamps a foot—sending flames dancing into the night. He lifts his arms in exultation. He throws back his head and laughs—the challenger, the conqueror laughs the first laugh of creation again and again and again.

Suddenly, in the middle of that blackest night, right at midnight, when stars, moons, and planets are utterly dimmed by enchantment, day comes. Light splits the darkness again. Day falls upon Enchanted City—shafts of glorious light, brilliant rays of brightness, dawning come untimely. And the King in the center of the burning field lifts his face to the warm new sun and at that, the flowering fire quiets and the King steps from the flames.

And all see at once that he is the meaning of the dance; he is the other side of the death place, his word weaves universe out of chaos; he is the restorer of all lost cities; his life is the potion all must take against enchantment.

The great crowd of subjects of the King ring Burning Place. A circle, a great vast circle, stretches around the dusty rim of the death field. They join hands, reaching to their neighbor, young to old, woman to man, adult to child. From the center of the burning flower, quieted but still luxuriant with light, the familiar music begins. It is the music of the Great Celebration. *Ah-h-h-h-h,* they have heard this before; *ah-h-h-h-h,* slowly, very slowly, the great circle begins to turn.

Hero watches the graceful movements. But the people are not changed. Is becoming over? *Will we never be real again, he wonders, become who we really are?*

"Hero!" a Ranger friend calls. "Are you no longer dancing?"

The music quickens as the King in the center stoops and lifts an armful of flame which shimmers and flutters in his embrace, alive. And as the dance passes, he tosses a flower to this one, to that until the whole moving ring is filled with brilliant light, like comets, like galaxies of orbiting moons. And Hero watches as each now becomes, not passing through the Circle of Sacred Flames, but being passed through themselves by holy light as the shining fires

179

disappear only to shine brightly from each one's eyes.

Then the King, the King himself, cries to Hero, "Keeper of the Chronicle! Light?" And when he turns his face, it is then that Hero sees the mark. A scar new from the burning, a scar like his own—but not like it. It is not the Enchanter's mark, not stamped into the flesh by hot iron. It is like a flower high on the cheekbone, like a crown, like a red and perfect rose. Lifting his hand to his face, Hero discovers that the rough fleshly rim of his own scar has disappeared. The mark of branding has been forever healed.

Overwhelmed, all Hero can do is laugh—the Enchantment truly is broken! And his feet, almost despite themselves, begin to step to the music, and he draws himself up proud, standing tall, a subject of the King, this most beautiful of men alive. And he is proud to be called a King's man.

"LIGHT!" he calls back.

The King tosses the dancing fire his way, and Hero's head is bathed in warmth as he feels the wonderful homespun wool of the cloak of Ranger blue falling around his shoulders, and he is lighted through and through. He breathes the sudden cool air of Great Park, fragrant with field and flower. He looks into the eye of street urchin and orphan, and they are truly beautiful. And his soul feels bold; at heart he knows he is a man of courage.

Nearby, Mercie's luxuriant black hair falls to her waist; she is once again the most beautiful of women. Ranger Commander, strong, broad shouldered and grand, bows to his warrior wife. Amanda, in her royal garments, dances in the ring way across the field. Hero watches as the circle moves closer, and he

180

sees the old gladsome laughter in her eyes. He meets
her to take her hand and to join the dance beside her
as they all, subjects of the Kingdom, laugh and sing
and step the sacred steps round and round this Most
Royal Highness, His Majesty the King.

*It is only then, when the circle is finally fulfilled, and
each one he loves has become real with sacred starshine
in their eyes, that the King himself turns in motion to
the sweet, solemn and glorious music of Great Park.
Then, while his own eyes shine with day, he lifts his
hands to the light, and in his first morning of the beginning again of all time, he proclaims aloud, "The
Enchantment is broken!*

"LET THE RESTORATION BEGIN!"

The young King lives, and so does his dream for the
world. With God all things are possible.

ON WITH THE RESTORATION!

The restoration has begun. The kingdom and kingship
will not be complete until our Lord returns in power and
glory and rules over all the earth. But even now we who
are marked by his fire, model for all to see a life of love
for God and others. We are the ones who, like "His
Majesty," treat others the way we would have them treat
us.

We say on his behalf, "Are you looking for compassion? For someone to put a loving arm around you as
you grieve? Are you searching for the people who will
treat you right, according to God's ways? Come, we'll do
our best to show you what that looks like."

No one is really inhibiting the church from being the

church in this land. That's true in many nations of the world. In Korea, Nigeria, India, Ukraine, Brazil, Australia, Japan, Mexico, even China—it's really difficult to stop believers from acting toward others in a Christlike way if that's what they are determined to do.

In this country, with all its freedoms, there has been a strange twist. It's as if the church here is surprised when our citizenry doesn't adhere to the ways of Christ. In our history, our society as a whole seldom, if ever, has truly followed Jesus. But I can hardly think of anyplace else in the world where Christians expect citizens or government leaders to do so. It would be wonderful if that happened, but it's hardly the norm. I doubt that Jesus expected Herod to convert. The church, not the government, was to be the light.

Hopefully, governments would understand it was to their advantage to have people around who consistently treated others in the way they themselves wanted to be treated.

In North America, some believers today sound more reactive than proactive. Rehearsing the bad news rather than living and sharing the Good News, they concentrate on the evils in our society, rather than seeing the increasing opportunities to show "kingslove." This is a barrier we must overcome. A reactive agenda won't capture this generation. Living out Christ's kingdom in their midst is what will win hearts.

Yes, our society is in bad shape. It's not as bad as some in the world, but even so, all around the globe, often in what would appear to be the most impossible of settings, the kingdom dream lives on and is doing fine. The church is alive with Resurrection fire. The day for spiritual heroics has hardly come to an end. In fact, revival is actually becoming increasingly common. As believers, let us dare to dream God's dreams again, his dreams for us as individuals and his dreams for the church. It's never too late to dream.

Are there dreams related to his righteous rule that the young King has birthed in your heart? What's a spiritual longing that you're earnestly praying will someday become a reality? Have you given God the option of healing your painful past and entrusting you with the new identity he's chosen for you? What current evidence have you written down that cites God's ongoing involvement in your life? Have you set any godly goals for the future? Are you learning to empower everything you do with prayer? Have you determined to confront your ungodly prejudices and widen your circle of unlikely friends? Who's someone you're attempting to excite about becoming a part of Christ's now-and-future kingdom? What's a part of the world you're praying will soon open up to His Majesty's touch? Are you letting God move you beyond your comfort zones? Do you hold a deep-seated conviction that with God all things are possible? Are you overcoming barriers that previously held you back? Are you daring to dream again?

How tragic it would have been for us if Christ had decided to give up his dreams for us. And how sad for

Jesus if his subjects are only excited about his righteous rule in the life to come but remain relatively uninterested in his plans for this present world.

It's time for God's dreams to be birthed in us again.

In *Tales of the Resistance*, an hourly cry is often shouted from one watch tower to another. "How goes the world? The world goes not well. But the Kingdom comes!"

We in North America need to begin each day with the good news that the young King lives and so does his dream for the world.

Whoever makes the coffee in the morning should call upstairs, "How goes the world?" Whoever hears the question should respond, "The world goes not well, but the kingdom comes!"

If you start your day watching "Good Morning America" with Diane Sawyer and Charlie Gibson, or "Today" with Matt Lauer and Katie Couric, you'll discover that as attractive as these people might be, they don't understand that the world goes not well but the kingdom comes. Start your day by reading the average newspaper, and you'll miss the all-important message of the kingdom.

But for those of us who bow before him, the young King lives, and his dream for the world lives as well.

So begin each day with this news! Rehearse it again on the morrow. Repeat it daily even as brave brothers and sisters do all around the world. This is a world which goes not well, but the kingdom comes. The enchantment is broken.

Now, on with the restoration!

FOR DISCUSSION AND REFLECTION

1. How much of Christ's message about his kingship or his kingdom do you identify with?

2. From your personal experience, would you say the church at large concentrates more on proclaiming good news or on emphasizing bad news?

3. How do you think the average non-Christian, who may only know from watching religious television, would answer the previous question?

4. Reflect on Christ's approach to ministry. Were there obvious evils he chose not to address? Did he primarily preach good news or bad news? Was his ministry proactive or reactive? Be prepared to defend your answer.

5. Without naming the ministry, evaluate an outreach you support financially or through your prayers. Is it more proactive or reactive?

6. How does the truth that all things are possible with God affect your service on his behalf?

185

Readings

It's time for the lambs to roar.

What I'm calling for is a radically different way of thinking about our world. Instead of running from it, we need to rush into it. And instead of just hanging around the fringes of our culture, we need to be right smack dab in the middle of it.

Why not believe that one day the most critically acclaimed director in Hollywood could be an active Christian layman in his church? Why not hope that the Pulitzer Prize for investigative reporting could go to a Christian journalist on staff at a major daily newspaper? Is it really too much of a stretch to think that a major exhibit at the Museum of Modern Art could feature the works of an artist on staff at one of our fine Christian colleges? Am I out of my mind to suggest that your son or daughter could be the principle dancer for the Joffrey Ballet Company, leading a weekly Bible study for the other dancers in what was once considered a profession that was morally bankrupt?

I don't think so. In fact, I believe it has been the pessimistic vision of the church that has prevented generations of young people from venturing out into the culture-shaping professions of our world. I've always wondered why we could be so quick to sacrifice our children to become missionaries but stand in the way of their becoming broadcast journalists, film and television actors, photographers, and painters. It's almost as if we believe God is strong enough to take care of his own only as long as they stay within the safety of the Christian ghetto. And yet, the Bible gives us countless examples of people like Joseph, who not only served as an advisor to the "president" of his day but also used that position to influence the entire land.

Can't we do that today? Shouldn't we be encouraging and equipping our sons and daughters to become Josephs too?

A friend of mine told me about a conversation he had with a member of his church. The two were talking about their frustration over their church's inability to have any impact on their community. It was a relatively small church—about 150 members—in an upscale suburban Midwest city. Included in the congregation were a leading surgeon, several business executives, a department head of a prestigious public school, as well as a number of lawyers, teachers, and sales reps. But, my friend observed, we're just sort of treading water. Things are getting worse in our community, families are breaking up, our kids aren't even accepting our faith, and we seem to waste so much time fighting with each other.

My friend then recalled the response of his fellow church member: "Don't you know, Jim, this is as good as it gets."

That church, like so many others, is filled with lambs who've lost their voice. Not only have they failed to

187

penetrate their community with their values, they have come to accept their failure as inevitable.

I believe it's not only possible but absolutely necessary for Christians and Christian values to become a vital element in the overall moral and cultural discourse of our nation. Without our strategic involvement in the culture-shaping arenas of art, entertainment, the media, education, and the like, this nation simply cannot be the great and glorious society it once was. If we are to be obedient to our Lord's call to go into all the world, we will begin reentering the fields that we have fled.

Are you ready to roar?

Roaring Lambs,
Bob Briner, Zondervan, pages 31–32.

•••

When Michael Korda wrote *Power! How to Get It, How to Use It,* his book quickly became a bestseller. Writing in a provocative, no-nonsense style, the author argued that life is a game of power: getting it, controlling it, and using it to obtain security, fame, sex, and money. After quoting Lord Acton's famous statement that "Power tends to corrupt and absolute power corrupts absolutely," Korda argued that it is worse to not push for power. We live in a world that is run by power, he wrote, and we need to grab it, hang on to it, enjoy it, and use it to get what we want.

Everybody knows about power struggles between husbands and wives, parents and children, rival street gangs, political foes, and opposing factions in universities, corporations, professional organizations, religious denominations, or churches. Most of these struggles involve self-centered actions, hard feelings, anger, and the manipulation of other people. The players in the power games feel anxiety and insecurity, even when they win the largest share of the power.

It is not easy to be a difference maker in a world, a community, or a family where people are struggling for power. Sometimes, we have to work with individuals (often incompetent and unreasonable individuals) who are jealous of their power and threatened when they learn about our difference-maker plans and passions. At times we must work within the power conscious system of local government. We may have to get approval for our buildings and plans from committees, church boards, or people in positions of power. Sometimes it seems difficult to maintain integrity when we have to live and work in a power-crazed culture. According to futurist Alvin Toffler, we are entering a period of history when "the entire structure of power that held the world together is now disintegrating." . . .

Despite these changes, however, we are not helpless pawns in the hands of others who hold power or struggle to get it. For centuries, committed and determined difference makers have been able to make significant changes, despite the power of others who get in the way. When God is leading us to make a difference, we can

189

move forward with confidence, especially when we remember two important truths: power can be destructive, but ultimate power belongs to God.

You Can Make a Difference,
Gary R. Collins, Zondervan, pages 236–237.

•••

Be still, my soul—thy God doth undertake
To guide the future as He has the past;
Thy hope, thy confidence let nothing shake—
All now mysterious shall be bright at last.
Be still, my soul—the waves and winds still know
His voice who ruled them while He dwelt below.

"Be Still My Soul,"
lyrics by Katharina von Schlegel,
Great Hymns of the Faith, Singspirtation, page 290.

EXPERIENCE THE ADVENTURES OF THE KINGDOM TALES TRILOGY!

If you have enjoyed reading the stories from *Tales of the Resistance,* you'll be excited to know that you can find out more about Hero, Amanda, and the story of Enchanted City in the complete Kingdom Tales trilogy. . . .

In the Gold Medallion Award-winning *Tales of the Kingdom,* discover how a frightened orphan named Scarboy flees Enchanted City and arrives at Great Park, where he meets Mercie, Caretaker, the Princess Amanda, and many others, and is finally changed by the King himself to become a Ranger with the new name of Hero.

Tales of the Resistance, another Gold Medallion Award winner, continues the story of Hero and his friends' efforts to overthrow the evil Enchanter and free Enchanted City's oppressed citizens. The third book, *Tales of the Restoration,* traces the journey of Hero and Amanda, Thespia, and the Grandma Vigilantes, as they begin to restore the kingship in the newly dubbed Bright City.

Enhanced with beautiful full-color illustrations and bound in hard cover, the Kingdom Tales make perfect gifts for your relatives and friends. Children of all ages will hear the message of Christ's kingdom through powerful allegory, and will be transformed by the deep biblical principles woven throughout every story.

See the next page for more details on *Tales of the Resistance.*

Visit **www.teamsundays.org** to view pictures or to order the entire trilogy.

Tales of the
RESISTANCE

Read the full story of the Taxi Resistance and discover exactly how Hero, Amanda, Big Operator, and the taxi drivers battle against the evil Enchanter and his merciless no-people to free hundreds of orphans.

Meet Carny, Sewer Rat, Boiler Brat, and other suffering citizens of Enchanted City and read the deeply moving stories of how they are rescued and healed by the King.

Experience these classic tales along with their full-color illustrations time and again. Order your Kingdom Tales copies today!

To order, call Mainstay Church Resources toll-free at 1-800-224-2735 (U.S.), 1-800-461-4114 (Canada). Or visit our website at www.teamsundays.org.